Janice VanCleave's

200

Gooey,
Slippery,
Slimy,
Weird,
and Fun
Experiments

Other Books by Janice VanCleave

Science for Every Kid Series
Janice VanCleave's Astronomy for Every Kid
Janice VanCleave's Biology for Every Kid
Janice VanCleave's Chemistry for Every Kid
Janice VanCleave's Dinosaurs for Every Kid
Janice VanCleave's Earth Science for Every Kid
Janice VanCleave's Ecology for Every Kid
Janice VanCleave's Geography for Every Kid
Janice VanCleave's Geometry for Every Kid
Janice VanCleave's The Human Body for Every Kid
Janice VanCleave's Math for Every Kid
Janice VanCleave's Oceans for Every Kid
Janice VanCleave's Physics for Every Kid

Spectacular Science Projects Series
Janice VanCleave's Animals
Janice VanCleave's Earthquakes
Janice VanCleave's Electricity
Janice VanCleave's Gravity
Janice VanCleave's Machines
Janice VanCleave's Magnets
Janice VanCleave's Microscopes and Magnifying Lenses
Janice VanCleave's Molecules
Janice VanCleave's Rocks and Minerals
Janice VanCleave's Volcanoes
Janice VanCleave's Weather

Janice VanCleave's 201 Awesome, Magical, Bizarre, and Incredible Experiments
Janice VanCleave's 202 Oozing, Bubbling, Dripping, and Bouncing Experiments

Janice VanCleave's

200

Gooey, Slippery, Slimy, Weird, and Fun Experiments

Janice VanCleave

JOSSEY-BASS
A Wiley Imprint
www.josseybass.com

Published by Jossey-Bass
A Wiley Imprint
989 Market Street, San Francisco, CA 94103-1741   www.josseybass.com

Jossey-Bass books and products are available through most bookstores. To contact Jossey-Bass directly call our Customer Care Department within the U.S. at 800-956-7739, outside the U.S. at 317-572-3986, or fax 317-572-4002.

Jossey-Bass also publishes its books in a variety of electronic formats. Some content that appears in print may not be available in electronic books.

Portions of this book have been reprinted from the books *Janice VanCleave's Biology for Every Kid*, *Janice VanCleave's Chemistry for Every Kid*, *Janice VanCleave's Earth Science for Every Kid*, *Janice VanCleave's Astronomy for Every Kid*, and *Janice VanCleave's Physics for Every Kid*, published by John Wiley & Sons, Inc.

The publisher and the author have made every reasonable effort to ensure that the experiments and activities in this book are safe when conducted as instructed but assume no responsibility for any damage caused or sustained while performing the experiments or activities in this book. Parents, guardians, and/or teachers should supervise young readers who undertake the experiments and activities in this book.

Library of Congress Cataloging-in-Publication Data

VanCleave, Janice Pratt.
  [200 gooey, slippery, slimy, weird, and fun experiments]
  Janice VanCleave's 200 gooey, slippery, slimy, weird, and fun
experiments.
      p.   cm.
    Includes index.
    Summary: Provides instructions for 200 experiments in biology,
chemistry, physics, earth science, and astronomy.
    ISBN 0-471-57921-1
    1. Science—Experiments—Juvenile literature.   2. Scientific
recreations—Juvenile literature.   [1. Science—Experiments.
2. Experiments.   3. Scientific recreations.]   I. Title.   II. Title:
200 gooey, slippery, slimy, weird, and fun experiments.   III. Title:
Two hundred gooey, slippery, slimy, weird, and fun experiments.
  Q164.V37   1992
  507'.8—dc20   92-15959

Printed in the United States of America
FIRST EDITION
PB Printing   30 29 28 27 26 25 24 23 22 21

Dedicated to an encouraging friend,
Ruth Roddam Ethridge

Introduction

This book is a collection of science experiments designed to show you that science is more than a list of facts—science is fun! The 200 experiments in the book take science out of the laboratory and put it into your daily life.

Science is a way of solving problems and discovering why things happen the way they do. Why does the Moon stay in orbit? How do you tell the age of a fish? Why are there holes in bread? You'll find the answers to these and many other questions by doing the experiments in this book.

The experiments cover five different fields of science:

- **Astronomy** The study of the planet we live on—Earth—and all our neighbors in space.
- **Biology** The study of the way living organisms behave and interact.
- **Chemistry** The study of the way materials are put together and their behavior under different conditions.
- **Earth Science** The study of the unique habitat that all known living creatures share—the Earth.
- **Physics** The study of energy and matter and the relationship between them.

The Experiments

Scientists identify a problem, or an event, and seek solutions, or explanations, through research and experimentation. A goal of this book is to guide you through the steps necessary to successfully complete a science experiment and to teach you the best method of solving problems and discovering answers.

1. **Purpose:** The basic goals for the experiment.
2. **Materials:** A list of necessary supplies.
3. **Procedure:** Step-by-step instructions on how to perform the experiment.
4. **Results:** An explanation stating exactly what is expected to happen. This is an immediate learning tool. If the expected results are achieved, the experimenter has an immediate positive reinforcement. An error is also quickly recognized, and the need to start over or make corrections is readily apparent.
5. **Why?** An explanation of why the results were achieved is described in terms that are understandable to the reader who may not be familiar with scientific terms. When a new term is introduced and explained, it appears in *italic* type; these terms can also be found in the Glossary.

You will be rewarded with successful experiments if you read an experiment carefully, follow each step in order, and do not substitute materials.

General Instructions

1. **Read first.** Read each experiment completely before starting.
2. **Collect needed supplies.** You will experience less frustration and more fun if all the necessary materials for the experiments are ready for instant use. You lose your train of thought when you have to stop and search for supplies.

3. **Experiment.** Follow each step very carefully, never skip steps, and do not add your own. Safety is of the utmost importance, and by reading the experiment before starting, then following the instructions exactly, you can feel confident that no unexpected results will occur.

4. **Observe.** If your results are not the same as described in the experiment, carefully read the instructions, and start over from the first step.

Measurements

Measuring quantities described in this book are intended to be those commonly used in every kitchen. When specific amounts are given, you need to use a measuring instrument closest to the described amount. The quantities listed are not critical, and a variation of very small amounts more or less will not alter the results.

Contents

I
Astronomy

1. Too Close

Purpose To determine how distance from the Sun affects atmospheric temperature.

Materials 2 thermometers   1 desk lamp
           yardstick (meter stick)

Procedure
- Place one thermometer on the 4 in. (10 cm) mark and the second thermometer on the 36 in. (100 cm) mark of the yardstick (meter stick).
- Position the lamp at the 0 end of the yardstick (meter stick).
- Turn the lamp on.
- Read and record the temperatures on both thermometers after 10 minutes.

Results The temperature is hotter on the closer thermometer.

Why? The thermometer closer to the lamp receives more energy and thus gets hotter. As the light moves away from the lamp, rays leaving at an angle do not hit the distant thermometer. The atmosphere of a planet is heated in a similar way. Mercury is the planet closest to the Sun and receives the most

energy. Planets farther from the Sun receive less heat and have cooler atmospheres. Mercury is much hotter than Pluto, which is very far from the Sun. Other factors such as density and pressure also affect the atmospheric temperature.

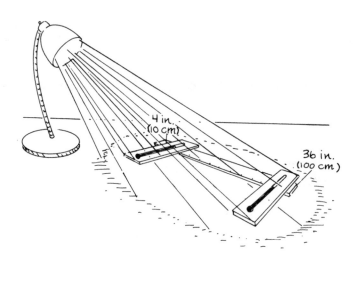

2. Quicker

Purpose To determine how distance affects a planet's period of revolution.

Materials modeling clay   ruler
           yardstick (meter stick)

Procedure
- Place a walnut-sized ball of clay on one end of the ruler and on one end of the yardstick (meter stick).
- Hold the yardstick and ruler vertically, side by side, with the edge without the clay ball on the ground.
- Release both at the same time.

Results The ruler hits the surface first.

Why? The clay ball on the yardstick has farther to fall than does the ball on the ruler. This is similar to the movement of the planets, which are continuously "falling" around the Sun. Mercury, with the shortest distance from the Sun, 36 million miles (57.96 million km), takes only 88 Earth days to make its voyage around the Sun. Pluto has a much longer path to follow—it is 3,688 million miles

(5,901 million km) away from the Sun and requires 248 Earth years to complete its period of *revolution* (time to move around the Sun).

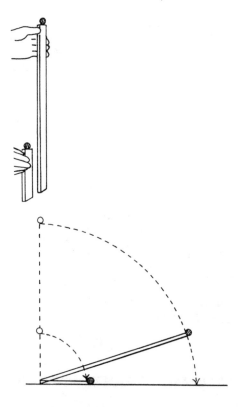

3. Blue Sky

Purpose To determine why the Earth is called the blue planet.

Materials drinking glass   milk
         flashlight   spoon
         eyedropper

Procedure
- Fill the glass with water.
- In a darkened room, use the flashlight to direct a light beam through the center of the water.
- Add 1 drop of milk to the water and stir.
- Again, shine the light through the water.

Results The light passes through the clear water, but the milky water has a pale blue-gray look.

Why? The waves of color in white light each have a different size. The particles of milk in the water separate and spread the small blue waves from the light throughout the water, causing the water to appear blue. Nitrogen and oxygen molecules in the Earth's atmosphere, like the milk particles, are small enough to separate out the small blue light waves from sunlight. The blue light spreads out through the atmosphere, making the sky look blue from the Earth and giving the entire planet a blue look when it is observed from space. The color in the glass is not a bright blue because more than just the blue light waves are being scattered by large particles in the milk. This happens in the atmosphere when large quantities of dust or water vapor scatter more than just the blue light waves. Clean, dry air produces the deepest blue sky color because the blue waves in the light are scattered the most.

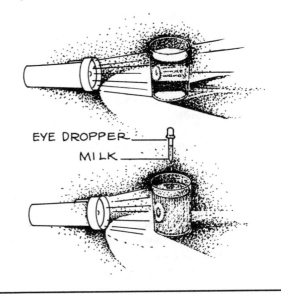

EYE DROPPER

MILK

4. Back Up

Purpose To demonstrate the apparent backward motion of Mars.

Materials helper

Procedure
- This is an outside activity.
- Ask a helper to stand next to you and then to start slowly walking forward.
- Look past your helper's head and notice the background objects that he or she passes.
- Start walking toward your helper at a faster speed than your helper.
- Continue to observe the background past your helper's head.
- Stop and ask your helper to stop when you are about 5 yd. (5 m) in front of him or her.

Results At first, you are looking forward to view the background past your helper, but as you take the lead you must look backward to see your helper and the objects beyond.

Why? Your helper is not going backward; you are simply looking from a different position. Mars was thought by early observers to move forward, stop, go backward, and then go forward again. Actually the planet was continuing forward on its *orbit* around the Sun while the Earth was zipping around the Sun in one-half the time of Mars' trip. Earth speeds ahead of Mars during part of the time, giving Mars the appearance of moving backward. Mars appears to move forward when the Earth races around the orbit and approaches Mars from behind. This apparent change in the direction of Mars is called *retrograde* motion.

5. Red Spot

Purpose To demonstrate the movement in Jupiter's red spot.

Materials wide-mouthed jar, 1 gal. (4 liters)
  1 tea bag
  pencil

Procedure
- Fill the jar with water.
- Open the tea bag and pour the tea leaves into the water.
- Insert the pencil into the center of the water.
- Move the pencil quickly in a small circle until the tea leaves group and begin to swirl in the center area of the water.

Results The tea leaves group in a spiraling funnel shape.

Why? The stirring creates a *vortex* (a mass of liquid or gas that whirls in the jar, forming a cavity in the center toward which things are pulled). The tea leaves are pulled toward the center of the vortex created by the rotating water. The red spot seen on Jupiter is a massive hurricane large enough to

swallow three Earths. It is believed that red particles are swirled by moving gases as were the tea leaves, creating the massive storm that has not changed in appearance for as long as people have been able to view Jupiter.

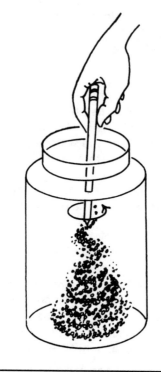

6. Glimmer

Purpose To determine why Jupiter's ring shines.

Materials flashlight
  baby powder in a plastic shaker

Procedure
- In a darkened room, place the flashlight on the edge of a table.
- Hold the open powder container below the beam of light.
- Quickly squeeze the powder container.

Results The beam of light is barely visible before the powder is sprayed into it. After spraying powder into the light beam, the specks of powder glisten, making the light path visible.

Why? Light is not visible unless it can be reflected to your eye. The tiny specks of powder act like the fine particles in the ring around Jupiter in that they reflect the Sun's light. Jupiter's ring is 34,000 miles (54,400 km) from the planet's cloud tops. The material in these rings is thought to come from Io, the innermost of Jupiter's four large moons. Io is the only known moon with active volcanoes, and it is

possible that the ash from these volcanoes forms Jupiter's ring.

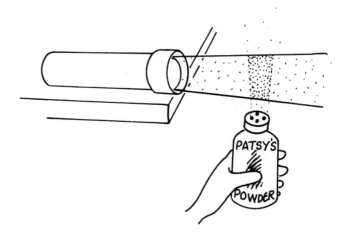

7. Hidden

Purpose To demonstrate how Mercury's position affects the observation of its surface.

Materials desk lamp   ruler
              pencil

Procedure
- Turn the lamp on with the glowing bulb facing you. Caution: Do not look directly into the lamp.
- Grasp the pencil in the center with the print on the pencil facing you.
- Hold the pencil at arm's length from your face and about 6 in. (15 cm) from the glowing bulb.

Results The print cannot be read on the pencil, and the color of the pencil is difficult to determine.

Why? The light behind the pencil is so bright that it is difficult to see the surface of the pencil. In a similar way, the glare of the Sun behind the planet Mercury makes it difficult to study the planet's surface. Mercury is less than half the size of the Earth and the closest planet to the Sun. From the Earth, astronomers are looking almost directly into the Sun when they view Mercury. The first photographs of one-third of the planet's surface were taken in 1974 and 1975 when the Mariner 10 space probe flew about 200 miles (320 km) from the surface of Mercury.

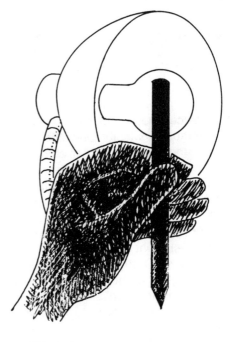

8. Big Red

Purpose To produce the material that causes the surface of Mars to have its red color.

Materials 1 paper towel   1 steel wool soap pad
              saucer   rubber gloves (like those
                                used to wash dishes)

Procedure
- Fold the paper towel in half twice and place it in the saucer.
- Run warm water from the faucet over the steel wool pad to remove as much of the soap as possible.
- Place the wet steel wool pad in the center of the paper towel in the saucer.
- Place the saucer where it will not be disturbed for 5 days.
- Observe the steel wool pad periodically during the 5 days.
- After 5 days, put on rubber gloves and pick the pad up and rub between your fingers.

Results The pad changes from a hard, silvery metal to a reddish powder.

Why? Steel wool contains the metal iron, which combines with oxygen in the air to form *rust* (a reddish powder). The soil on Mars is composed mostly of the elements silicon and oxygen mixed with metals including iron and magnesium. An abundance of iron oxide, the combination of iron and oxygen that is called rust, gives Mars its reddish color. Storms in the thin atmosphere of the planet cause winds to swirl the red dust and sand, which form a red cloud that covers the surface of Mars for weeks and months at a time.

SAUCER

FOLDED PAPER TOWEL

9. Peeper

Purpose To determine when the planet Mercury is the most visible from Earth.

Materials cellophane tape   black marking pen
desk lamp   basketball
yardstick (meter stick)

Procedure
- Center a piece of tape across the opening of a desk lamp. The tape should not touch the light bulb.
- Use a marking pen to mark a small dot on the tape above the center of the light bulb.
- Position the lamp so that the bulb faces you.
- Turn the light on and stand 1 yd. (1 m) in front of the bulb.
- Close your left eye and look at the dot on the tape with your open right eye.
- Slowly move your body to the left until the dot appears just slightly to the right of the light bulb.
- Stand in this position while holding a basketball in front of your face. Continue to keep your left eye closed.
- Move the ball so that it blocks your view of the light bulb but allows you to see the dot on the tape.

Results The dot is easily seen when it is to the side of the bulb and the basketball blocks out the light from the bulb.

Why? The planet Mercury can be seen from the Earth with your naked eye just before the Sun rises in the morning and sets below the horizon in the afternoon. The basketball in this experiment represents the horizon of the Earth, the dot is Mercury, and the light bulb is the Sun. The position of these materials demonstrates that only when the Sun's blinding light is below the Earth's horizon can the planet Mercury peep above the horizon and be seen easily.

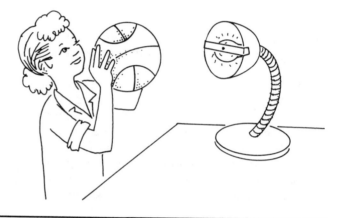

10. Curves

Purpose To demonstrate the effect of forces on orbital movement.

Materials 2 chairs   small paper cup
masking tape   poster board
yardstick (meter stick)   (dark color)
scissors   salt
string   pencil

Procedure
- Separate the chairs and tape the ends of the yardstick to the top edge of each chair's back.
- Cut two 1-yd. (1-m) lengths of string.
- Attach both ends of one string to the yardstick to form a V-shaped support. Secure the ends with tape.
- Loop the second string over the V-shaped string and use tape to attach the ends to the top rim of the cup, one on each side of the cup. Tie so that the cup is about 4 in. (10 cm) from the floor.
- Lay the poster board under the hanging cup.
- Fill the cup with salt.
- Use the point of a pencil to make a small hole in the bottom of the cup.
- Pull the cup back and release to allow it to swing forward.

Results The falling salt forms different patterns on the dark paper as the cup swings.

Why? The cup moves in different patterns because of the forces pulling on the cup. The cup was swung in a back and forth motion, the V-shaped support string pulled it in another direction, and there is the ever-present downward pull of gravity. Planets, like the cup, have different forces acting on them. Each planet spins on its axis and has a forward speed and is pulled on by other planets and its own moon(s), but the big pull is from the Sun. The combination of all of these forces guides the planet in the path (*orbit*) it takes around the Sun.

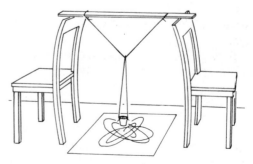

11. Elliptical

Purpose To determine how gravity affects the movement of celestial bodies.

Materials 1 sheet of typing paper
1 sheet of carbon paper
clipboard
modeling clay
cardboard tube from paper towel roll
large glass marble

Procedure

■ Place the typing paper on the clipboard.
■ Lay the carbon paper on top of the typing paper, carbon side down.
■ Place both sheets under the clip on the board.
■ Raise the clip end of the board by placing two marble-sized balls of clay under both corners.
■ Place one end of the paper tube on top of the papers.
■ The tube should be parallel with the top of the clipboard.
■ Slightly elevate the tube by placing a ball of clay under one end.
■ Place the marble in the elevated end of the tube and allow it to roll out of the tube and across the papers.
■ Raise the carbon sheet and observe the pattern produced on the typing paper.

Results The pattern made by the marble is curved. *Note:* Change the elevation if the marble's path is not curved.

Why? The marble has a horizontal speed and would continue to move straight across the paper if gravity did not pull it downward. The forward force plus the downward pull moves the marble in a curved path. The paths of planets are also affected by the gravitational pull of the Sun. All the planets have forward motions as well as a pull toward the Sun. If the Sun had no gravitational attraction, the planets would not orbit the Sun, but would move away from the Sun in a straight line.

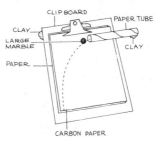

12. Satellite Crash

Purpose To demonstrate why a satellite stays in orbit.

Materials poster board   large, empty, 3-lb.
       pencil   (1.4-kg) coffee can
       ruler   masking tape
       scissors   glass marble

Procedure

■ On the poster board, draw a circle with a 22 in. (55 cm) diameter.
■ Cut around the circle, then cut out a wedge (pie slice) that is one-eighth of the circle.
■ Overlap the circle to form a cone that fits snugly in the coffee can with most of the cone sticking out the top of the can. Tape the cone so it does not open up.
■ Tape the cone to the outside of the can.
■ Roll the marble around the top of the cone as fast as possible and observe its movement.

Results The marble rolls around the inside of the cone and its path begins to curve downward as the speed of the marble slows. The marble finally moves to the bottom of the cone and stops.

Why? The paper offers a continuous resistance to the movement of the marble, forcing it to move in a circular path, and gravity pulls the marble downward. As the forward speed of the marble decreases, the unchanging pull of gravity forces the marble to move down the cone toward the bottom. Satellites would continue to circle the Earth if they never lost their forward motion, but like the marble, as their speed decreases, gravity pulls them toward the Earth until finally they crash into the Earth. Planets and moons are examples of satellites since they all orbit another celestial body; they would crash if their forward speed decreased.

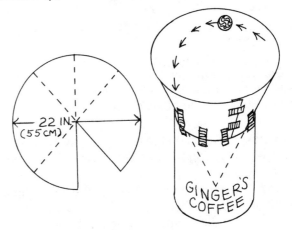

13. Orbiter

Purpose To demonstrate the force that keeps satellites in orbit around the Earth.

Materials small-mouthed glass jar, 1 pint (500 ml)
marble

Procedure
- Use your hand to hold the jar horizontally with its opening pointing to the side.
- Place a marble inside the jar.
- Gently place the mouth of the jar against the palm of your other hand.
- Move the jar around in a circular path until the marble quickly spins around on the inside of the jar.
- Continue to move the jar around as you slowly turn the jar and your palm upside down. You may have to practice this movement to keep the marble moving at a constant speed.
- Remove your palm from the mouth of the jar.
- Stop moving the jar.

Results The marble remains inside the jar as long as the jar is spun. The marble continues to spin for a short time after you stop moving the jar, but finally the marble slows and falls out of the jar.

Why? The jar pushes on the marble and provides an inward force that keeps the marble moving in a circular path. This force toward the center is called a *centripetal force*. The word centripetal means "seeking the center." If the bottle were suddenly removed, the marble would fly off in a straight line because of its forward speed.

Any object moving in a circular path—the marble, a moon, or an artificial satellite—has a forward speed and a centripetal force pulling it inward. The Earth's natural and artificial satellites are pulled toward the Earth's surface by gravity, but their own forward speed keeps them from being pulled into the Earth. Satellites, like the marble, fall when their forward speed decreases.

14. Shut Out

Purpose To demonstrate the effect a lunar eclipse has on studying the Sun's corona.

Materials index card   desk lamp
                straight pin

Procedure
Caution: NEVER look at the Sun directly because it can damage your eyes.
- Use the straight pin to make a hole in the center of the card.
- Slightly hollow out the hole so that you can see through it.
- Turn the lamp on.
- Close your right eye.
- Hold the card in front of your left eye.
- Look through the pinhole at the glowing lamp.

Results The print on the outside of the bulb can be read when looking through the pinhole.

Why? The card shuts out most of the light from the bulb, allowing the print to be visible. During a solar eclipse, the Moon blocks the glaring light from the

Sun, allowing the less intense glowing outer surface, or *corona*, to be studied.

PINHOLE

15. Trapped

Purpose To determine how the Earth is protected from solar winds.

Materials bar magnet
2 sheets of notebook paper
iron filings, as found in magnetic
   disguise games
drinking straw

Procedure
- Cover the magnet with one sheet of paper.
- Fold the second sheet of paper and sprinkle iron filings in the fold.
- Hold the paper about 6 in. (15 cm) from the magnet.
- Blow through the straw.
- Direct the stream of air at the iron filings in the folded paper. A stream of iron filings are blown toward the magnet.

Results Particles of iron stick to the paper in the shape of the underlying magnet.

Why? Around the magnet is a *magnetic force field* that attracts the iron filings. The Earth has a magnetic force field surrounding it. The area affected by the magnetic field is called the *magnetosphere*. The magnetosphere deflects and traps charged particles from the Sun, much as the magnet under the paper attracted the iron filings. The charged particles come from the Sun as a result of solar flares and sunspots. These moving particles are called solar winds and reach the Earth's orbit at speeds up to 1 to 2 million miles/hr (1.6 to 3.2 million km/hr). Astronauts in space could be in danger from solar flare particles because the high-energy particles damage living tissue. Without the Earth's magnetosphere, living organisms on the Earth would be in danger from the charged particles.

16. Riser

Purpose To determine how the Sun can be seen before it rises above the horizon.

Materials 1 clear glass jar with a lid, 1 qt. (1 liter)
   table   books
   ruler   modeling clay

Procedure
- Fill the jar to overflowing with water.
- Tightly screw the lid on the jar.
- Lay the jar on its side on a table about 12 in. (30 cm) from the edge of the table.
- On the edge of the table in front of the jar, stack books so that about one-fourth of the jar rises above the books.
- Make a ball of clay about the size of a walnut.
- Lay the clay ball on the table about 4 in. (10 cm) from the jar.
- Kneel down in front of the books.
- Look straight across the top surface of the books and through the jar of water. If the clay ball is not visible, move it to a new position.
- Keeping your head in this position, move the jar out of your line of vision.

Results You can see the clay ball only by looking through the jar of water.

Why? Looking through the jar of water allows you to see the clay ball even though it is below the level of the top of the books. Everything you look at is seen because light from that object reaches your eye. The light from the clay ball passed through the jar and was *refracted* (bent) toward your eye. Light from objects in the sky passes through the Earth's *atmosphere* (hundreds of miles of air surrounding the Earth) before reaching your eyes. The Earth's atmosphere causes light to be refracted in the same way as does the jar of water. Because of the refraction of light, you see the Sun a few minutes before it actually rises above the horizon in the morning and for a few minutes after it sets in the afternoon.

17. Bright Spot

Purpose To safely observe the image of the Sun.

Materials 1 large box—the author used a box 12
in. × 12 in. × 24 in. (30 cm × 30
cm × 60 cm)

scissors   masking tape
binoculars   aluminum foil
index card   1 sheet of typing paper

Procedure

Caution: NEVER look at the Sun directly because it
can damage your eyes.

- Turn the box so that its opening is facing to the side.
- Cut a hole in the top side of a box just large enough
  for the small ends of the binoculars to fit into.
- Cut out a circle from an index card. Tape the paper
  circle over one of the large ends of the binoculars.
- Fit the binoculars into the space cut in the top of the
  box with the small ends down. Secure with tape.
- Wrap pieces of aluminum foil around the binoculars
  to seal any open spaces between the binoculars and the box.
- Set the box outside in a sunny area and sit in front
  of the open side.

- Tilt the box so that the open lens of the binoculars
  points toward the sun and no shadow of the binoculars falls on top of the box. DO NOT LOOK
  DIRECTLY AT THE SUN.
- Hold a sheet of typing paper inside the box, and
  while looking at the paper, move the paper up and
  down until the image of the Sun is clearly seen on
  the paper.

Results A bright circle of light is seen on the paper.

Why? The Sun's brilliant light can permanently damage your eyes, so a special instrument must be used
to see the image of the Sun's surface and not the actual surface. The open lens in the binoculars focuses
the light from the Sun onto the paper screen, and
thus the Sun's image can be safely observed.

18. Packed

Purpose To demonstrate why the Sun's center has
a greater density (mass of a specific volume) than
the outside.

Materials 1 bag miniature marshmallows, 1 lb.
(454 g)
plastic cup, 16 oz. (480 ml)
food scale

Procedure

- Drop marshmallows into a plastic cup one at a
  time until the marshmallows are even with the top
  of the cup.
- Use a food scale to measure the weight of the cup
  of marshmallows.
- Remove the cup from the scale and place it on a
  table.
- With your fingers, push the marshmallows in the
  cup down into the cup.
- Refill the empty space in the cup with marshmallows and again push the marshmallows down to
  make room for more.
- Continue to add and press the marshmallows
  down until no more can be added and the marshmallows are even with the top of the cup.

- Use the food scale again to measure the weight of
  the cup.

Results The cup with the pressed marshmallows
weighs more.

Why? The cup has a constant *volume* (space occupied by matter) and is filled each time with the same
material, marshmallows. The cup and its content of
marshmallows weigh more when more marshmallows are pressed into the cup. This experiment
demonstrates why the *core* (center) of the Sun has a
greater density than the outside. *Density* is the scientific way of comparing the "heaviness" of materials; it is a measurement of the mass (weight) of a
specific volume. The Sun is believed to be made of
the same material throughout, but samples of the
same volume would weigh more if taken near the
Sun's center. The Sun's *gravity* (pull toward the center) is very great, so the materials near the core are
pressed together; therefore the density is greater.

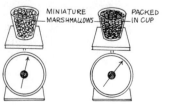

19. Flaming Colors

Purpose To determine the colors that make up white light from the Sun.

Materials shallow baking pan
flat pocket mirror
1 sheet white typing paper

Procedure

Caution: This experiment must be done on a sunny day, and you must not look directly at the Sun or use the mirror to reflect the Sun's light toward another person's eyes.

- Fill a shallow baking pan with water.
- Place the pan on a table near a window so that it receives the morning sunlight.
- Place a flat mirror inside the pan so that it rests at an angle against one side of the pan.
- With one hand, hold a sheet of white paper in front of the mirror.
- Use your other hand to move the mirror slightly. Adjust the position of the mirror and paper until a rainbow of colors appears on the white paper.
- Slightly shake the mirror.

Results Flickering rainbow-colored flames appear on the white paper.

Why? The layer of water between the mirror and the surface of the water acts like a *prism*. A prism is a triangle-shaped piece of glass that bends the rays of light passing through it so that the light breaks into its separate colors, called a *spectrum*. The white light of the Sun can be separated by a prism into a spectrum of seven colors always appearing in the same order: red, orange, yellow, green, blue, indigo, and violet. The moving water changes the direction of the light, causing the colors to appear like flickering flames.

20. Night Lights

Purpose To simulate and describe the attraction of charged particles near the Earth's poles.

Materials paper hole punch
tissue paper
table
round balloon, small enough to hold in your hand when inflated
your own hair—be sure it is clean, dry, and oil-free

Procedure

- Punch 20 to 30 holes out of the tissue paper with the hole punch.
- Place the paper circles on a table.
- Stroke the balloon against your hair 10 times.
- Hold the stroked side of the balloon near, but not touching, the paper circles.

Results The paper circles jump toward the balloon. Some of the circles leap off the balloon.

Why? The paper circles represent charged particles circling the Earth at great distances, and the balloon represents the Earth. As was explained in Experiment 15, the Earth has a *magnetosphere* around it that deflects and traps charged particles from the Sun. The poles of the Earth act like strong magnets and pull some of the charged particles from the magnetosphere toward the Earth. Unlike the paper circles, the charged particles do not hit and leap from the Earth's surface, but move around in the upper atmosphere near the poles, bumping into the atoms of gas in the atmosphere. The gas atoms become excited when hit by these charged particles and release visible light. Each type of atom emits a specific color, resulting in a spectacular light display. The light display in the Northern Hemisphere is called an *aurora borealis* and in the Southern Hemisphere an *aurora australis*.

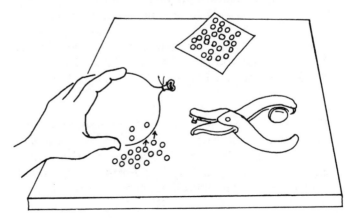

21. Spinner

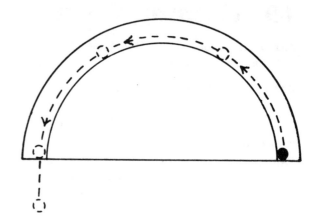

Purpose To demonstrate why the Moon stays in orbit.

Materials paper plate   marble
scissors

Procedure
- Cut the paper plate in half and use one side.
- Place the marble on the cut edge of the plate.
- Set the plate down on a table and slightly tilt it so that the marble moves quickly around the groove in the plate.

Results The marble leaves the plate and moves in a straight line away from the paper plate.

Why? Objects move in a straight path unless some force pushes or pulls on them. The marble moved in a circular path while on the plate because the paper continued to push the marble toward the center of the plate. As soon as the paper ended, the marble traveled in a straight line. The Moon has a forward speed and, like the marble, would move off in a straight line if the gravitational pull toward the Earth did not keep it in its circular path.

22. Face Forward

Purpose To demonstrate that the Moon rotates on its axis.

Materials 2 sheets of paper   masking tape
marker

Procedure
- Draw a circle in the center of one sheet of paper.
- Write the word EARTH in the center of the circle, and place the paper on the floor.
- Mark a large X in the center of the second sheet of paper, and tape this paper to a wall.
- Stand by the side of the paper on the floor and face the X on the wall.
- Walk around the Earth, but continue to face the X.
- Turn so that you face the paper labeled EARTH.
- Walk around the Earth, but continue to face the Earth.

Results Facing the X-marked paper resulted in different parts of your body pointing toward the paper marked EARTH as you revolved around the Earth. Continuing to face the Earth allowed only your front side to point toward the Earth during the revolution.

Why? You had to turn your body slightly in order to continue to face the Earth as you moved around it. In order for the same side of the Moon to always face the Earth, the Moon also has to turn slowly on its axis as it moves around the Earth. The moon rotates one complete turn on its own axis during the 28 days its takes to revolve around the Earth.

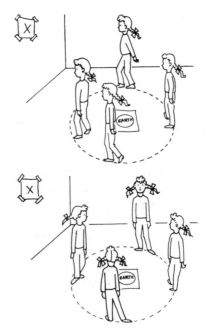

23. Faces

Purpose To determine the cause of the "Man in the Moon" image.

Materials dominoes   flashlight
                    table

Procedure
- Stand 6 to 8 dominoes on a table.
- Darken the room and hold a flashlight at an angle about 12 in. (30 cm) from the dominoes.

Results The dominoes form shadows on the table.

Why? The dominoes block the light from the flashlight much as the mountainous regions on the Moon, called *highlands,* block the Sun's light. The shadows of the highlands fall across the flat plains, called *maria.* The highlands look brighter, as they reflect the light, and the maria look darker because of the shadows. The insides of craters on the Moon also appear dark. The combination of highlands, maria, and craters forms the "Man in the Moon" pattern on the surface of the Moon.

24. Star Clock

Purpose To determine why the stars seem to move in circles across the night sky.

Materials umbrella, solid, dark color   white chalk

Procedure
- Use chalk to draw the stars in the Big Dipper on one of the panels inside the umbrella. Draw the entire constellation.
- Hold the umbrella over your head.
- Turn the handle slowly in a counterclockwise direction.

Results The center of the umbrella stays in the same place, and the stars move around.

Why? The stars in the constellation called the Big Dipper appear to move around a central star like hands on a backward clock. The stars make one complete turn every 24 hours, but unlike a clock, the hands are not in the same position each night at the same time. The stars reach a given position about 4 minutes earlier each night. Actually, the stars are not moving, we are. The Earth makes one complete rotation every 24 hours, making the stars appear to move. The axis of the Earth points to Polaris, the North Star, and it is this star that all the other stars appear to move around.

BIG DIPPER

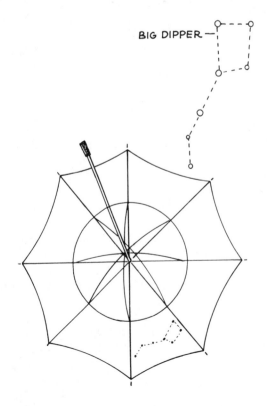

25. Daytime Stars

Purpose To demonstrate that the stars are always shining.

Materials paper hole punch
index card
1 white letter envelope
flashlight

Procedure
- Cut 7 to 8 holes in the index card with the hole punch.
- Insert the index card in the envelope.
- In a well-lighted room, hold the envelope in front of you with the flashlight about 2 in. (5 cm) from the front of the envelope and over the index card.
- Move the flashlight behind the envelope.
- Hold the flashlight about 2 in. (5 cm) from the back of the envelope.

Results The holes in the index card are not seen when the light shines on the front side of the envelope, but are easily seen when the light comes from behind the envelope and toward you.

Why? Light from the room passes through the holes in the card regardless of the position of the flashlight, but only when the surrounding area is darker than the light coming through the holes can they be seen. This is also true of stars. They shine during the daylight hours, but the sky is so bright from the Sun's light that the starlight just blends in. Stars are most visible on a moonless night in areas away from city lights.

26. Streaks

Purpose To determine why stars appear to rotate.

Materials black construction paper   white chalk
scissors   pencil
ruler   masking tape

Procedure
- Cut a circle with a 6-in. (15-cm) diameter from the black paper.
- Use chalk to randomly place 10 small dots on the black circle.
- Insert the point of the pencil through the center of the paper.
- Use tape to secure the pencil to the underside of the paper circle.
- Twirl the pencil back and forth between the palms of your hands.

Results Rings of light appear on the spinning paper.

Why? Your mind retains the image of the chalk dots as the paper spins, causing the paper to appear to have rings on it. A similar picture is produced when astronomers expose photographic plates under starlight for several hours. The light from the stars continuously affects the exposed film, producing streaks as if the stars were moving in a circular path. The truth is that the stars are relatively stationary and the Earth is moving. The stars just appear to move around in the sky, but actually the film is moving with the Earth as it spins on its axis.

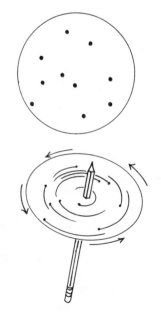

27. Box Planetarium

Purpose To demonstrate how planetariums produce images of the night sky.

Materials
shoe box	black construction paper
scissors	cellophane tape
flashlight	straight pin

Procedure
- Cut a square from the end of the shoe box.
- At the other end of the box, cut a circle just large enough to insert the end of the flashlight.
- Cover the square opening with a piece of black paper. Secure the paper to the box with tape.
- Use the pin to make 7 to 8 holes in the black paper.
- Point the shoe box toward a blank wall.
- In a darkened room, turn on the flashlight.
- Move back and forth from the wall to form clear images of small light spots on the wall. Make the holes in the black paper larger if the spots on the wall are too small.

Results An enlarged pattern of the holes made in the paper is projected onto the wall.

Why? As light beams shine through the tiny holes, they spread outward, producing larger circles of light on the wall. A planetarium presentation showing the entire night sky uses a round sphere with holes spaced in the positions of single stars and *constellations.* A constellation is a group of stars whose arrangement forms an imaginary figure. A bright light in the center of the sphere projects light spots on a curved ceiling, representing the sky. As the ball rotates, different star groups are seen. Because of the Earth's revolution around the Sun, different stars are viewed in the sky at different times of the year.

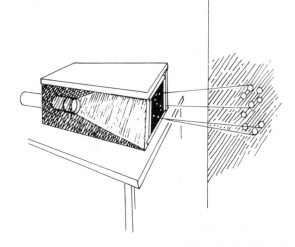

28. Spirals

Purpose To demonstrate the movement of a spiral galaxy.

Materials
jar, 1 qt. (1 liter)	paper hole punch
1 sheet of notebook paper	pencil

Procedure
- Fill the jar about three-fourths full with water.
- Cut about 20 circles from the paper with the hole punch.
- Sprinkle the paper circles on the surface of the water.
- Quickly stir the water in a circular motion with a pencil.
- View the water from the top and sides after you stop stirring.

Results The paper circles swirl around, forming a spiral shape in the center.

Why? The spinning paper only simulates the spiral movement and concentration of material of a star-studded *spiral galaxy.* Galaxies are thicker in the center; they actually bulge. The Milky Way galaxy is a spiral galaxy. It takes the Milky Way 250 million years to make one complete turn, but much space is covered during this rotation by the more than 200 billion stars. Our solar system is just a small part of this large spiraling mass that is 100,000 light years from edge to edge. A light year is a measure of distance, not time. One light year means that it takes light, traveling at a speed of 186,000 miles (300,000 km) per second, one entire year to travel the distance.

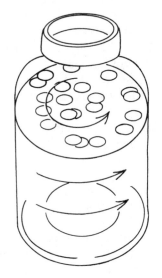

29. Inverted

Purpose To demonstrate how light travels through the lens of a refractive telescope.

Materials dark construction paper, 1 sheet
scissors
gooseneck desk lamp
masking tape
ruler
magnifying lens

Procedure

■ Cut a paper circle from the dark paper to fit the opening of the lamp.
■ Cut an arrow design in the center of the paper circle.
■ Tape the circle over the lamp.

Caution: Be sure that the paper does not rest on the lightbulb. The bulb will get hot.

■ Place the lamp about 6 ft. (2 m) from a wall.
■ Turn the lamp on, and darken the rest of the room.
■ Hold the magnifying lens about 12 in. (30 cm) from the lamp.
■ Move the magnifying lens back and forth from the lamp until a clear image is projected on the wall.

Results The image produced on the wall is turned upside down.

Why? Light travels in a straight line, but when it hits the lens, it changes direction, causing the image to be upside down. Refractive telescopes have lenses similar to the one used in this experiment, and so stars viewed through a refractive telescope appear upside down.

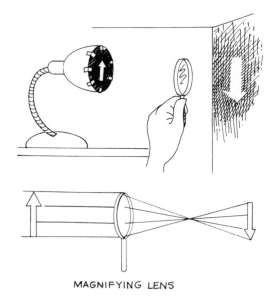

MAGNIFYING LENS

30. Space Balance

Purpose To determine how mass can be measured in space.

Materials hacksaw blade, 10 in. (25.5 cm)
4 coins, any size
masking tape

Procedure

Caution: Have an adult cover the teeth of the blade with a strip of masking tape.

■ Tape the blade to the edge of a table.
■ Pull the free end of the blade back and release it.
■ Observe the speed at which the blade moves.
■ Use tape to attach two coins to the end of the blade, one on each side.
■ Pull the blade back as before and release it.
■ Attach two more coins to the blade and swing the blade as before.

Results As more coins are added, the speed of the swinging blade decreases.

Why? The swinging blade is called an *inertia balance.* Because the back-and-forth swing of the blade is the same in and out of a gravity field, the balance can be used as a measuring tool in space. *Inertia* is that property of matter by which it resists any sudden change in its state of motion or rest. As the mass of an object increases, the object's inertia increases. Therefore, it is more difficult to move a large mass. You applied the same amount of energy to each swing, but as the mass increased, it took more energy to move it. The number of swings for a specific mass could be determined, and by counting the number of swings, the mass of an object can be calculated.

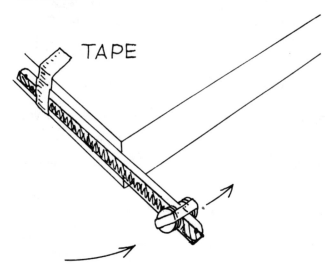

TAPE

31. Retroreflector

Purpose To determine how to measure the distance to the Moon.

Materials masking tape   sheet of notebook paper
2 flat mirrors   flashlight
table

Procedure
- The experiment should be performed in a room that can be darkened.
- Tape the edge of the mirrors together so that they open and close like a book.
- Stand the mirrors on a table.
- Tape the paper to the front of your shirt to form a screen.
- Place the flashlight on the table so that the light strikes one of the mirrors at an angle.
- Change the angle of the second mirror to find a position that reflects the light back to the screen on your shirt.

Results A ring of light appears on the paper screen.

Why? The light was reflected from one mirror to

another before bouncing back to the paper screen. The *retroreflector* left on the Moon was a set of mirrors similar to the ones in this experiment. The amount of time it took for a laser beam from Earth to reflect off the two and a half feet square retroreflector was measured and the distance from the Earth to the Moon calculated.

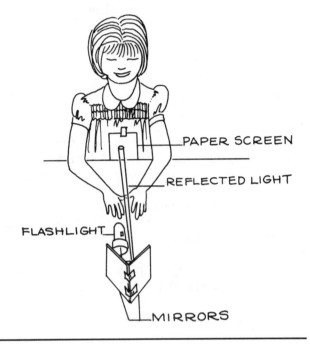

32. How High?

Purpose To determine how distance can be compared using an astrolabe.

Materials string   heavy bolt
scissors   drinking straw
ruler   masking tape
protractor   helper

Procedure
- Measure and cut a 12-in. (30-cm) piece of string.
- Tie one end of the string to the center of the protractor and attach the bolt to the other end of the string.
- Tape the straw along the top edge of the protractor.
- Look through the straw (keeping one eye closed) at the tops of distant objects and have your helper determine the angle of the hanging string.

Results The angle increases as the height of the objects increases.

Why? To see the tops of the distant objects, the protractor had to be elevated. The hanging string remains perpendicular to the ground because gravity continues to pull it toward the center of the Earth. As

the protractor turns, the string has a different angle in relation to the straw. This instrument is called an *astrolabe* and can be used to compare the distances between stars, since the distance increases as the angle increases.

33. Light Meter

Purpose   To demonstrate how to measure the brightness of light.

Materials   yardstick (meter stick)
small box such as a shoe box
aluminum foil
wax paper
scissors
cellophane tape
flashlight

Procedure

- Cut a large window in both ends of the box and two large windows in one side of the box.
- Cover the openings with four layers of wax paper. Secure the paper with tape.
- Fold a piece of aluminum so that it hangs in the center of the inside of the box, dividing the box. Secure the foil with tape.
- Put the lid on.
- In a darkened room, set the box on the floor and place the flashlight about 2 yd. (2 m) from the end of the box.
- Observe the side windows.

- Move the flashlight to 1 yd. (1 m) then ½ yd. (½ m) from the box's end.

Results   The side facing the light gets brighter as the light nears the box.

Why?   The aluminum foil reflects the light and the wax paper scatters it, causing the side facing the flashlight to be brighter. The brightness increases as the light source nears the box. The box is an example of a *photometer,* an instrument used to measure the brightness of a light. A more sensitive photoelectric meter can be used to measure the brightness of light from stars. A star closer to the Earth is much brighter than one of equal energy that is farther away.

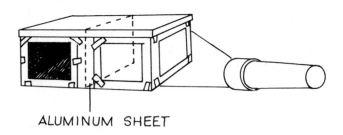

ALUMINUM SHEET

---

34. Bouncer

Purpose   To demonstrate how communication satellites work.

Materials   flat mirror   helper
modeling clay   flashlight
table

Procedure

- Use the clay to stand the mirror on a table positioned near an open door.
- Have a person stand in the next room so that he or she can see the mirror, but not see you.
- Shine the flashlight on the surface of the mirror.
- You and your helper need to find a position that allows the light to reflect from the mirror so that your helper sees the light, but does not see you.

Results   The light beam is sent from one room and seen by a person in another room.

Why?   The shiny surface of the mirror reflects the light. Radio waves, like the light, can be reflected from smooth surfaces and directed to receivers at different places around the world. A signal sent to an

orbiting satellite is bounced back at an angle to a receiver many miles away from the sender.

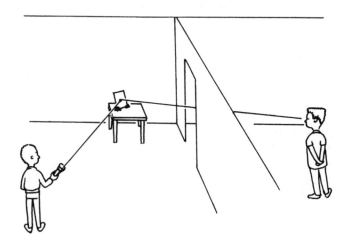

35. Staging

Purpose To demonstrate rocket staging.

Materials paper cup, 5 oz. (150 ml)
scissors
long balloon, 18 in. (45 cm)
round balloon, 9 in. (23 cm)

Procedure
- Cut the bottom from the paper cup.
- Partially inflate the long balloon and pull the open end of the balloon through the top and out the bottom of the cup.
- Fold the top of the balloon over the edge of the cup to keep the air from escaping as you place the round balloon inside the cup and inflate it.
- Release the mouth of the round balloon.

Results The attached balloons move forward quickly as the round balloon deflates. The cup falls away and the final balloon speeds forward as it deflates.

Why? The set of balloons represents a three-stage rocket. Great amounts of fuel are needed to lift and move heavy spacecraft. Each stage of the rocket system has its own set of engines and fuel supply.

As each stage uses up its fuel, it drops away, making the rocket system lighter. Each stage lifts the craft until finally the payload is put into orbit or achieves a fast enough speed to leave the Earth's atmosphere for a trip into space.

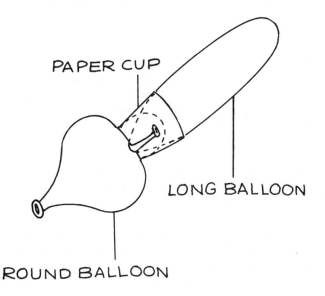

36. Flash!

Purpose To determine how crystal light might benefit space travel.

Materials wintergreen candy   wooden block
plastic sandwich bag   hammer

Procedure
Note: This experiment must be performed in a dark room. A closed closet works well.
- Place one wintergreen candy in the plastic bag.
- Place the bag on the wooden block.
- Position the hammer above the candy.
- Look directly at the candy piece as you smash it with the hammer.

Results A quick bluish-green flash of light is given off at the moment the candy crushes.

Why? Crystals broken by pressure give off light. This light is an example of *triboluminescence*. Crystals such as sugar and quartz give off light flashes when crushed. Crystals that give off light under pressure could possibly be used by engineers in designing the outer shield of space vehicles. It is possible that

instruments on Earth could detect crystal light flashes that would indicate trouble spots.

37. Darkness

Purpose To demonstrate why space is dark.

Materials flashlight   ruler
             table

Procedure
- Place the flashlight on the edge of a table.
- Darken the room, leaving only the flashlight on.
- Look at the beam of light leaving the flashlight and try to follow it across the room.
- Hold your hand about 12 in. (30 cm) from the end of the flashlight.

Results A circular light pattern forms on your hand, but little or no light is seen between the flashlight and your hand.

Why? Your hand reflected the light to your eyes, making the beam visible. Space is dark even though the Sun's light continuously passes through it because there is nothing to reflect the light to your eyes. Light is seen only when it is reflected from an object to your eyes.

38. Stop!

Purpose To demonstrate how gravity affects inertia.

Materials cereal (your choice)   bowl
             milk   spoon

Procedure
- Pour your favorite cereal into a bowl and add milk.
- Eat a spoonful of cereal.
- Raise a second spoonful of cereal to your mouth, but stop before putting the food in your mouth.
- Observe the position of the spoon and its contents.

Results When the spoon is stopped, the food stays in the spoon.

Why? This experiment does not present any mystifying results. Of course the food stays in the spoon, but is that always true? No! If you were eating in space and stopped the spoon before it reached your mouth, you would receive a face full of food. Gravity is pulling down with enough force to keep the food from moving forward when the spoon stops moving. *Inertia* means that an object in motion continues to move until stopped by some force. In space, the inertia of the food would keep it moving after the spoon had been stopped.

39. Sweaty

Purpose To determine what happens to water inside a closed area like a space suit.

Materials jar with a lid

Procedure
- Cover the bottom of the jar with water.
- Close the lid.
- Place the jar in direct sunlight for 2 hours.

Results Moisture collects on the inside of the jar.

Why? Heat from the Sun causes the surface water molecules inside the jar to *evaporate* (change from a liquid to a gas). When the gas hits the cool surface of the jar, it *condenses* (changes from a gas to a liquid). Human beings release salty water through the pores of their skin—perspire. The water from perspiration would evaporate and condense on different parts of the suit, as did the water inside the jar, until the entire inside of the suit was wet and uncomfortable. To prevent this, dry air enters through tubes at one part of the suit, and wet air, along with excess body heat, exits through another tube in a different part of the suit. This circulation of air provides a

cool, dry environment inside the extravehicular mobility unit—the space suit.

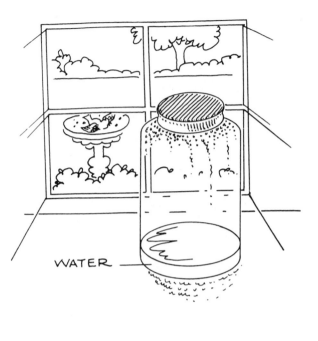

WATER

40. Tumbler

Purpose To demonstrate three kinds of satellite movements; roll, pitch, and yaw.

Materials modeling clay
3 colored toothpicks—red, blue, and green
index card
marking pen
scissors

Procedure
- Use modeling clay to form a spacecraft. The length, width, and height of your space vehicle must be less than the length of the toothpicks.
- Insert the red toothpick through the center of the craft from front to back. This is toothpick A in the diagram.
- Push the blue toothpick, toothpick B, through the approximate center of the craft from side to side.
- Stick toothpick C, the green stick, through the spacecraft's approximate center from top to bottom.
- Draw and cut out a small astronaut from an index card.
- Stick the paper astronaut into the clay at the top of the spacecraft as indicated in the diagram.

- With your hands, hold the ends of toothpick A.
- Roll the stick back and forth between your fingers.
- Observe the movement of the craft and the other toothpicks.
- In turn, hold the other two toothpicks rolling them back and forth between your fingers.
- Again observe the movement of the astronaut and spacecraft as the vehicle rotates.

Results The astronaut and spacecraft rotate around three different axes.

Why? The three different movements are called roll, pitch, and yaw. Turning around Axis A is called a roll. When the craft turns around Axis B, the movement is called pitch. Turning around Axis C is called yaw. Roll, pitch, and yaw are terms used to describe the motion of a spacecraft. These same terms are also used to describe the movements of airplanes, boats, or cars.

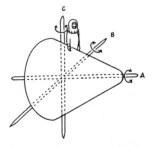

II
Biology

41. Spicy Escape

Purpose To demonstrate diffusion and osmosis.

Materials eyedropper   balloon, a small size
              vanilla extract   shoe box

Procedure
- Place 15 drops of vanilla extract inside the deflated balloon. Be careful not to get any of the vanilla on the outside of the balloon.
- Inflate the balloon to a size that will comfortably fit inside the shoe box and tie the open end.
- Place the balloon in the empty shoe box. Leave the balloon in the closed box for 1 hour.
- Open the box and smell the air inside.

Results The air smells like vanilla. The box is still dry.

Why? The balloon appears to be solid, but it actually has very small invisible holes all over its surface. The liquid vanilla molecules are too large to pass through the holes, but the molecules of vanilla vapor are smaller than the holes and pass through. The movement of the vapor through the rubber membrane is called diffusion.

The escaped vanilla vapor moves throughout the air in the shoe box and, once the box is open, through the air in the room. This spontaneous movement of molecules from one place to another is called diffusion. If you wait long enough, the diffusion will result in a uniform mixture of the vanilla vapors and the air with which it mixes.

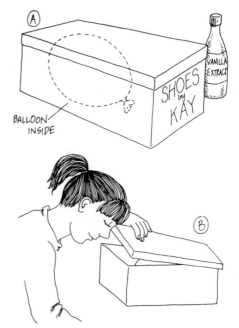

42. Fluffy Raisins

Purpose To observe the effect of osmosis on a raisin.

Materials glass of water   10 to 12 raisins

Procedure
- Place the raisins in the glass of water.
- Allow them to stand overnight.

Results The raisins swell, and become fluffy and smooth.

Why? During osmosis, water moves from a greater concentration through a membrane to an area of lesser water concentration. The raisins were dry inside, thus the water in the glass moved through the cell membranes into the raisins. As the cells filled with water, the raisins became plump and fluffy.

43. Stand Up

Purpose To demonstrate how the change in turgor pressure causes plant stems to wilt.

Materials wilted stalk of celery
1 drinking glass
blue food coloring

Procedure
- Ask an adult to cut a slice from the bottom of a wilted celery stalk.
- Put enough food coloring into a glass half full of water to turn it dark blue.
- Allow the celery to stand overnight in the blue water.

Results The celery leaves become a blue-green color, and the stalk is firm and crisp.

Why? A fresh cut across the bottom insures that the celery cells are not closed off or dried out. Water enters into the water-conducting tubes called *xylem.* These tubes run the length of the stalk of the celery. Water leaves the xylem tubes and enters the cells up and down the celery stalk. Plants usually stand erect and return to their original position when gently bent.

This happens because each plant cell is normally full of water. The water makes each cell firm, and all the cells together cause the plant to be rigid. A plant wilts when it is deprived of water, and like half-filled balloons, the cells collapse, causing leaves and stems to droop. The pressure of the water inside the plant cell is called *turgor pressure.*

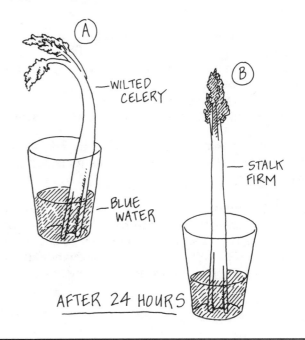

AFTER 24 HOURS

44. Leaf Straw

Purpose To demonstrate that the leaves and stems of plants can act like a straw.

Materials glass soda bottle   pencil
ivy leaf and stem   straw
clay   mirror

Procedure
- Fill the bottle with water to within an inch of its top.
- Wrap the clay around the stem near the leaf.
- Place the stem into the bottle. The end of the stem must be below the surface of the water.
- Cover the mouth of the bottle with the clay.
- Push the pencil through the clay to make an opening for the straw.
- Insert the straw so that its opening is in the air space at the top of the bottle.
- Squeeze the clay around the straw.
- Stand in front of the mirror and look at the mirror image of the bottle while you suck the air out of the bottle through the straw. This should be difficult if there are no leaks in the clay, so use a lot of suction.

Results Bubbles start forming at the bottom of the stem.

Why? There are holes in the leaf called *stomata,* and tiny tubes called *xylem* run down the stem. The leaf and stem acted like a straw. As you sucked air out of the straw, more was drawn in through the leaf straw. It is through these tubes and holes that water moves in a plant.

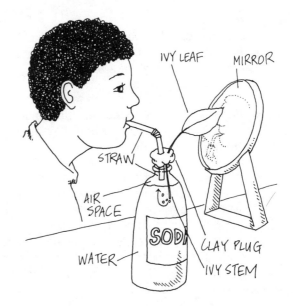

45. What's Stomata?

Purpose To determine which side of the plant leaf takes in gases.

Materials potted plant   Vaseline

Procedure
- Coat the top of four leaves with a heavy layer of Vaseline.
- Coat the underside of four leaves with a heavy layer of Vaseline.
- Observe the leaves daily for 1 week.
- Is there any difference in the two sets of leaves?

Results The leaves that had Vaseline coated on the underside died. The other leaves remained unchanged.

Why? Openings on the underside of plant leaves called *stomata* allow gases to move into and out of the leaves. The Vaseline plugged the openings and the leaf was not able to receive necessary carbon dioxide gas or eliminate excess oxygen gas.

46. Water Loss

Purpose To demonstrate transpiration, the loss of water from leaves.

Materials growing plant
plastic sandwich bag
tape (cellophane)

Procedure
- Place the sandwich bag over one leaf.
- Secure the bag to the stem with the tape.
- Place the plant in sunlight for 2 to 3 hours.
- Observe the inside of the bag.

Results Droplets of water collect on the inside of the plastic bag. The inside of the bag may appear cloudy due to the water in the air.

Why? Plants absorb water from the soil through their roots. This water moves up the stem to the leaves, where 90 percent is lost through the pores of the leaf (stomata). Some trees lose as much as 15,000 pounds (6,818 kg) of water within a 12-hour period. Plants can greatly affect the temperature and humidity of a heavily vegetated area. This loss of water through the stomata of the leaves is called *transpiration*.

47. Independence

Purpose To demonstrate the independence of plants.

Materials 1-gallon (4-liter) jar with a large mouth and lid
small pot plant

Procedure
- Moisten the soil of the plant.
- Place the entire plant, pot and all, inside the gallon jar.
- Close the jar with its lid.
- Place the jar somewhere that receives sunlight for part of the day.
- Leave the jar closed for 30 days.

Results Periodically, drops of water will be seen on the inside of the jar. The plant continues to grow.

Why? The water drops come from the moisture in the soil and from the plant leaves. Plants use the sugar in their cells plus oxygen from the air to produce carbon dioxide, water, and energy. This is called the *respiration* reaction. They can use the carbon dioxide, water, chlorophyll, and light energy in their cells to produce sugar and oxygen. This process is called *photosynthesis.* Notice that the products of the respiration reaction fuel the photosynthesis reaction and vice versa. Plants continue to make their own food. They eventually die in the closed bottle because the nutrients in the soil are used up.

48. Up or Down?

Purpose To observe the effects of gravity on plant growth.

Materials houseplant   books

Procedure
- Lay the pot on its side on the books.
- Observe the position of the stem and leaves for 1 week.

Results The stem and leaves turn upward.

Why? Plants contain a chemical called auxin. Auxin causes plant cells to grow extra long. Gravity pulls the plant chemical downward so that along the bottom of the stem there is a buildup of auxin. The cells grow longer where the auxin buildup is, causing the stem to turn upward.

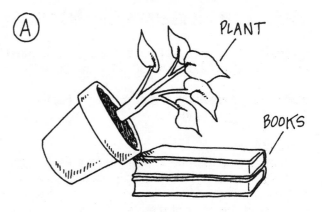

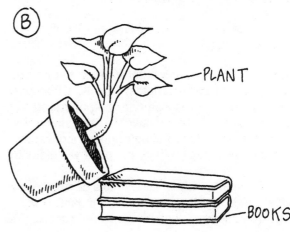

49. Light Seekers

Purpose To determine if plants do seek the light.

Materials houseplant

Procedure
- Place the plant next to a window for 3 days.
- Rotate the plant 180° and allow it to stand for another 3 days.

Results The leaves of the plant turn toward the window. Rotating the plant changes the direction of the leaves, but within three days they turn back toward the light.

Why? Plants contain a chemical called auxin that promotes the lengthening of plant cells. A buildup of auxin occurs on the dark side of the plant stem. The extra auxin causes the cells on the dark side to grow longer, forcing the stems to bend toward the light. This movement toward light is called *phototropism*. Photo means light and tropism means movement.

50. Darkness Below

Purpose To demonstrate why green plant life does not occur below 300 feet (100 m) in the ocean.

Materials 2 small green potted plants (same variety)

Procedure
- Place one of the plants in a sunny area, and the other plant in a dark closet or cabinet.
- Leave the plants for 7 days.
- Compare the color of the plants.

Results The plant in the closet will be lighter in color and wilted.

Why? Plants need sunlight to undergo the energy-making reaction called photosynthesis. Chlorophyll is a green pigment necessary in the photosynthesis reaction. Without the sunlight, the chlorophyll molecules are used up and not replenished, causing the plant to look pale. In time, the plant will die without sunlight.

Green plants grow in the ocean to a depth of about 300 feet (100 m). They are more abundant near the surface and decrease with an increase in depth. The concentration of sunlight is greatest at the surface and totally disappears below 300 feet (100 m). Green plants cannot live below 300 feet (100 m).

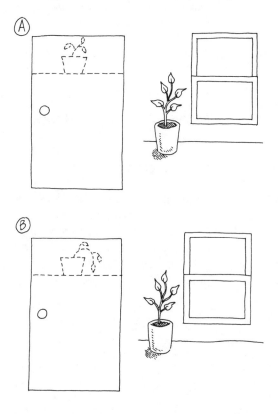

51. Veggie Plant

Purpose To grow plants from carrot tops.

Materials sand
shallow container
carrot tops (ask an adult to cut the tops
from several carrots)

Procedure
- Fill the container with sand.
- Thoroughly wet the sand with water.
- Insert the cut end of the carrot tops in the wet sand.
- Place in a lighted area.
- Keep the sand wet for 7 days.
- Observe the tops of the carrots for changes.

Results Tiny green stems and leaves begin to grow.

Why? The carrot top has the base of the stem and a portion of the root on it. All the necessary parts for a productive plant are present. The carrot portion is the root and contains the food reserve for the plant. Supplying the plant with water allows the stem to grow and produce leaves.

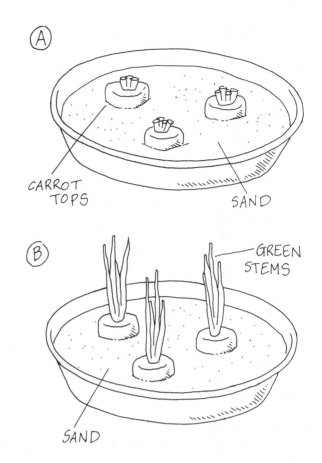

52. Protection

Purpose To demonstrate how water protects plants from freezing temperatures.

Materials 2 thermometers   2 saucers
aluminum foil   refrigerator
paper towels

Procedure
- Fold pieces of aluminum foil to make a holder for the thermometers. Loosely cover each thermometer with foil, leaving an opening at one end so it can be easily removed.
- Wrap two dry paper towels around each of the aluminum pouches.
- Wet the paper around one of the thermometers with water. Do not get water down inside the aluminum holder.
- Lay each covered thermometer on a saucer and place them in the freezer of a refrigerator.
- Read and record the temperature on each thermometer after 2 minutes.
- Continue reading and recording the temperature on each thermometer every 2 minutes for a total of 10 minutes.

Results The readings on the thermometer inside the holder covered with wet paper are higher.

Why? Changing the water in the paper towel from a liquid to a solid is called a *phase change*. A phase change requires a change in heat energy. When water freezes, it gives off energy to change from its liquid phase to its solid phase. As indicated by the difference in the thermometer readings, this lost energy heats up the area surrounding the changing water. Plants can be protected from freezing weather by spraying them with water. This method of protecting plants is not successful during prolonged freezing temperatures or when the air temperature drops below the freezing temperature of water.

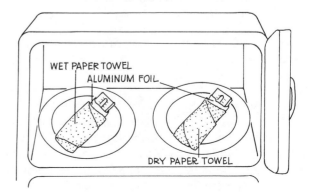

53. Morning Glory

Purpose To demonstrate how some flowers open quickly.

Materials newspaper   scissors
          marking pen   large bowl
          ruler

Procedure
- Draw a flower on a sheet of newspaper by following these instructions:
  - Draw a 6-in. (15-cm) diameter circle on the paper.
  - Draw four lines to divide the circle into eight equal parts.
  - Use the lines as a guide to draw flower petals as in the diagram.
- Cut out the paper flower.
- Fold each petal toward the center of the flower and crease it so that it lays flat. The petals will overlap.
- Fill the bowl with water.
- Place the folded paper flower, petal side up, on top of the water in the bowl.

Results The petals rise and the entire flower opens and floats on the surface of the water.

Why? The pressure of water inside the cells of plants is called *turgor pressure.* Morning glories are among a few types of flowers that open and close because of changes in the amount of water inside their cells. Turgor movements are usually rapid, occurring within 1 to 2 seconds or, at the most, 30 minutes. Water movement through the petals of morning glories as in the paper flower of this experiment is due to *capillary action* (the rising of water in small tubes). Plants, like paper, have tubes and tubelike structures through which water can move. As the water enters, the turgor pressure produced causes the structure to spread open.

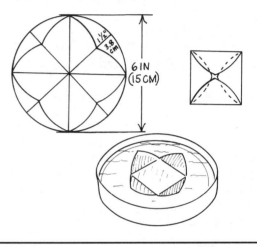

54. Bread Mold

Purpose To grow a type of fungus called bread mold.

Materials Ziploc® bag   eyedropper
          bread slice

Procedure
- Place the bread in the plastic bag.
- Put 10 drops of water inside the bag.
- Close the bag.
- Keep the bag in a dark, warm place for 3 to 5 days.
- Observe the bread through the plastic.
- Discard the bag and its contents after your observation.

Results A black, hairy-looking structure is growing on the bread.

Why? Mold is a form of fungus. It can grow and reproduce very quickly. Mold produces very tiny cells with hard coverings called *spores.* Spores are smaller than dust particles and float through the air. The slice of bread already has spores on it when placed in the plastic bag. The water, warmth, and darkness provide a good environment for the mold to grow.

Molds have good and bad effects. Some forms of mold make foods taste and smell bad, but there are foods that depend on mold for their good taste. Many cheeses are moldy and taste good. The greenish mold that forms on bread and oranges is used to make a medicine called penicillin.

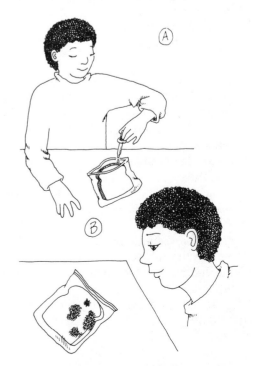

55. Hungry Fungus

Purpose To observe the effect that yeast has on a sugar solution.

Materials 1 package of powdered yeast
sugar
measuring spoon—tablespoon (15 ml)
measuring cup (250 ml)
glass soda bottle—16 oz (480 ml)
10-inch (25 cm) balloon

Procedure
- Mix the package of yeast and 1 spoon of sugar in one cup of warm water. Be sure the water is warm, not hot.
- Pour the solution into the soda bottle.
- Add another cup of warm water to the bottle.
- Squeeze the air out of the balloon and place it over the mouth of the bottle.
- Place the bottle in a warm, dark place for 3 to 4 days.
- Observe the bottle daily.

Results Bubbles are continuously being formed in the liquid. The balloon is partially inflated.

Why? Yeast is a fungus. It has no chlorophyll like other plants and cannot produce its own food. Like animals, yeast can use food such as sugar to produce energy. The yeast causes the sugar to change into alcohol, carbon dioxide gas, and energy. The bubbles observed in this experiment are carbon dioxide. This same gas causes bread to rise during baking as the bubbles push the moist dough up and outward. Gas holes can be seen in the finished bread. The nice smell from the baking of yeast bread is partially due to the evaporation of the alcohol produced.

56. Bacterial Growth

Purpose To demonstrate the effect that temperature has on the growth of bacteria.

Materials milk
measuring cup (250 ml)
2 pint (500 ml) jars
refrigerator

Procedure
- Put a cup of milk in each jar.
- Close each jar.
- Place one jar in the refrigerator.
- Place the second jar in a warm place.
- Examine the milk in each jar once a day for 7 days.

Results The warm milk has thick, white lumps in it and smells sour. The cold milk looks and smells like drinkable milk.

Why? Warm temperatures promote the growth of bacteria that can cause food to spoil. Cooler temperatures slow down the bacteria growth, but milk will eventually spoil if left in the refrigerator long enough. The bacteria are present and grow very slowly when cold, but they do grow.

WARM MILK   COLD MILK

57. Fireflies

Purpose To determine if the light from fireflies gives off heat.

Materials fireflies
2 glass jars with lids
2 thermometers (must fit inside the jars)

Procedure

- On a night when fireflies are plentiful, catch as many as you can and place them in a jar. It is easiest to catch them with your hands after they land on a surface.
- Put a thermometer into the jar with the fireflies and another thermometer in the empty jar.
- Record the temperature of each jar after 30 minutes.

Results Depending on the number of fireflies in the jar, the temperature may be slightly higher in the jar with the insects.

Why? The luminescence, or cold light, produced by the fireflies gives off no heat. Any rise in temperature in the jar is just due to body heat given off by the insects. The light produced by living organisms is called *bioluminescence*. The light is caused by the chemical luciferin. When this chemical combines with oxygen it gives off light. The color intensity and length of time between flashes depends on the species.

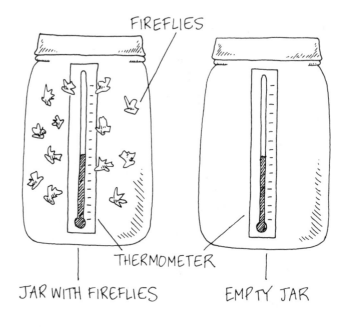

FIREFLIES

THERMOMETER

JAR WITH FIREFLIES   EMPTY JAR

58. Fly Trap

Purpose To observe the life cycle of a fly.

Materials banana   nylon stocking
1 quart jar (1 liter)   rubber band

Procedure

- Peel the banana and place the fruit inside the open jar.
- Leave the jar open and undisturbed for 3 to 5 days.
- Observe the jar daily. When 5 to 10 small fruit flies are seen inside the jar, cover the top with the stocking.
- Secure the stocking over the mouth of the jar with a rubber band.
- Leave the flies in the jar for 3 days, then release all of them.
- Re-cover the jar with the stocking.
- Observe the jar for 2 weeks.

Results Within a few days, maggots can be seen crawling around. Later, small capsules replace the maggots, and finally, new flies emerge.

Why? The fruit flies are attracted to the smell of the ripening fruit. The flies laid eggs on the fruit, and the eggs developed into the larvae, called maggots. The maggots go through a resting stage called the pupae. Pupae are similar to the cocoon formed by caterpillars. The last stage is the emerging adult fly and the cycle starts over again.

(A) OPEN JAR

FRUIT FLIES

PEELED BANANA

BANANA PEEL

(B) STOCKING

RUBBER BAND

MAGGOTS

59. Fish Rings

A — SUMMER GROWTH
— WINTER GROWTH

Purpose To determine the age of a fish.

Materials fish scales (collect fish scales from a local fish market)
dark paper
hand lens

Procedure
- Place a dried scale on the dark paper.
- Using the hand lens, study the ring pattern on the scale.
- Count the wide, lighter bands.

Results The number of wide bands equals the age of the fish in years.

Why? Like rings on a tree trunk, fish scales form rings with each year of growth. The rings grow fastest in warm weather when there is an abundance of food. During this growing season, the growth band is lighter in color and much wider than during the colder months of winter. The winter growth produces dark slim bands because the growth is so very slow. The ring pattern varies in design from one species to another.

B

FISH SCALES

HAND LENS

DARK PAPER

60. Holding On

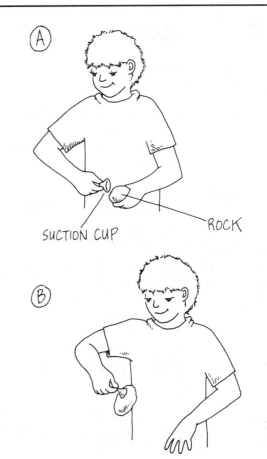

A

SUCTION CUP

ROCK

Purpose To demonstrate how some sea organisms, such as sea anemones, secure themselves to rocks.

Materials suction cup (the type used to secure hanging crafts to windows works well)
rock

Procedure
- Wet the suction cup and press it against the rock.
- Pick the rock up by holding onto the suction cup.

Results The suction cup sticks so securely that the rock can be lifted.

Why? Pressing the cup against the rock forces the air out of the cup. The water forms a seal around the outside, preventing the air from reentering the cup. The air in the room actually pushes with so much force on the outside of the cup that it is held tightly against the rock. The suction cups on sea anemones work the same way. Under the water, the suction cups on the organisms are held tightly against rocks by the pressure of the water.

B

61. Heads or Tails

Purpose To determine if one end of an earthworm is more sensitive to odors.

Materials earthworms (purchase at a bait shop or dig up your own)
paper towel
cotton balls
fingernail polish remover

Procedure
- Place several worms on a paper towel moistened with water.
- Wet the cotton ball with fingernail polish remover.
- Hold the wet cotton ball near, but not touching, the front or head end of the worm. This will be the end closest to the wide band around the worm's body.
- How does the worm respond to the odor?
- Hold the wet cotton near, but not touching, the tail end of the worm.
- Is there any difference in the response?
- Try holding the wet cotton near, but not touching, other sections of the worm's body.

Results The worm shows no area of greater sensitivity to the odor on the cotton ball. The worm makes an effort to move away from the irritating smell no matter where the cotton is placed.

Why? Earthworms do not have obvious sense organs, such as a nose, but they do have a nervous system that responds to stimuli such as odors. They have a brain at the front end of the body with a large nerve cord extending all the way to the tail. Each body segment also has a mass of nerve tissue that controls activities within the segment. This is why the worm responds to odor at any place on its body.

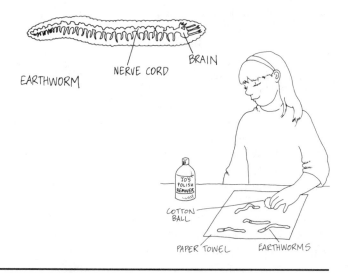

62. Floaters

Purpose To determine why earthworms surface during a heavy rain.

Materials container of earthworms and soil (can be purchased at a bait shop)
one-half cup (125 ml) of aquarium gravel (purchase at a pet store)

Procedure
- Pour water into the cup containing the gravel until the water covers the gravel.
- Explain why there are bubbles in the water. Why do they stop forming?
- Pour water into the container of earthworms and soil until the soil is covered.
- Did bubbles rise from the soil? How did the earthworms respond to the water?

Results Bubbles rise for a short time when water is added to gravel or soil. The earthworms rise to the top of the wet soil.

Why? The water pushed the air out of the cavities in the gravel, and since there are air spaces in the soil, the air was replaced by the water in the soil. The bubbles seen were air bubbles, and they stopped when all of the air was displaced by the water. The worms surfaced because of the lack of or low level of oxygen in the soil. During heavy rains, worms are often seen on the surface of soil—they are seeking oxygen.

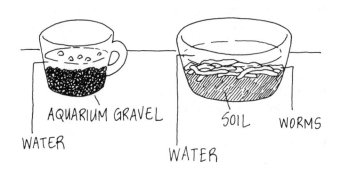

63. Hidden Picture

Purpose To observe the camouflaging technique of animals.

Materials pale yellow crayon
white typing paper
red, transparent, plastic folder

Procedure
- Draw a bird on the white paper with the yellow crayon.
- Cover the drawing with the red folder.

Results The yellow bird disappears.

Why? The yellow bird and the red folder are both reflecting light to your eyes. The red is not a pure color, but has some yellow in it. This yellow blends in with the yellow from the bird drawing, and your eye is not sensitive enough to separate them. Animals that have colorations similar to those of their environment are often camouflaged, hidden, from predators. The stalking animal's eyes cannot distinguish the colors well enough to separate its meal from the leaves.

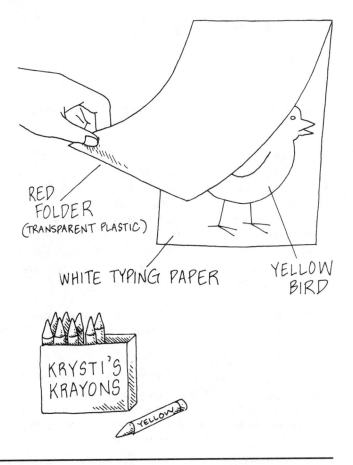

RED FOLDER (TRANSPARENT PLASTIC)

WHITE TYPING PAPER

YELLOW BIRD

KRYSTI'S KRAYONS

YELLOW

64. Water Breath

Purpose To explain how camels can live in the desert for weeks without drinking water.

Materials hand mirror

Procedure
- Breathe onto the mirror.

Results The mirror becomes fogged with tiny droplets of water.

Why? The exhaled breath of humans as well as camels contains water vapor. Some of the water in breath goes into the air, and some remains in the passages inside the nose. The passage inside the human nose is short and relatively straight. The camel's nose has long, twisting passages. Most of the water in a camel's breath stays inside the nose instead of escaping into the air. This allows camels to go longer without drinking because they do not lose as much water through their exhaled breath.

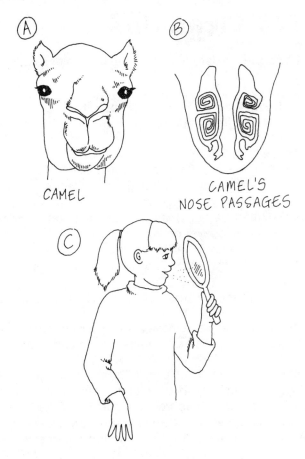

(A) CAMEL

(B) CAMEL'S NOSE PASSAGES

(C)

65. Inside Out

Purpose To demonstrate how snakes shed their skin.

Materials glove—a leather or rubber glove works best

Procedure
- Put a glove on one of your hands.
- Use your free hand to hold the top of the glove.
- Slowly start pulling your hand out of the glove.
- Move your holding hand to different sides of the glove as you pull your hand out of the glove.
- Make an effort to apply pressure with your fingers on the inside of the glove so that as they are pulled out the glove is turned inside out.

Results Your hand is free from its glove covering, and most if not all of the glove is turned inside out.

Why? Pulling the glove from your hand is very similar to the way a snake sheds its skin. You needed something to hold the glove as you pulled your hand out. A snake must first break the skin around its mouth and nose by rubbing its head on the ground or other rough surface. Once the skin on its head is loosened, the snake finds a rock or stick to hold the edge of the skin while it very slowly crawls out. The old inside-out skin is left behind as the snake moves away.

Snakes shed because their skin wears out or becomes too small. As a snake grows, a new, larger skin covering forms and the older, smaller outside skin is removed. Young snakes shed more often than older snakes because they are growing and are also more active and wear their skin out more quickly.

66. Clean Up

Purpose To determine how the tongue of a cat can clean the cat's fur.

Materials cotton ball   pencil
fingernail file

Procedure
- Rub the side of the sharpened end of a pencil across the end of your finger to collect a layer of graphite on your fingertip.
- Gently rub a fingernail file back and forth across the graphite layer on your finger.
- Observe your fingertip and the file.
- Rub the fingernail file back and forth across a cotton ball.
- Observe the surface of the cotton ball and the file.

Results The file removes the graphite from your fingertip and pulls loose fibers off the cotton ball.

Why? The rough surface of the file rubs the loose layer of graphite off your finger and catches and pulls the loose fibers from the surface of the cotton ball. This experiment demonstrates how a rough surface can be used to clean another surface. A cat licks its fur to clean it. Its tongue feels like coarse sandpaper because of the tough pieces of skin, called papillae, sticking up in the center. These bristles of flesh act just like the ridges on the fingernail file. When the cat rubs its coat with its tongue, the papillae remove dust, dirt, and loose hair.

67. Big to Little

Purpose To observe the effect that light has on the size of an eye pupil.

Materials mirror

Procedure
- Sit in a brightly lighted room for 2 minutes.
- Keep one eye tightly closed and the other eye open.
- Observe the pupil of the open eye by looking in the mirror. (The pupil is the dark spot in the center of the eye.)
- Open the closed eye and immediately observe the size of the pupil.
- Notice any size changes in the pupil as the eye remains open.

Results The pupil in the open eye is very small compared with the pupil of the eye that had been closed. The larger pupil shrinks within seconds after the eye is exposed to the light.

Why? In dim light or darkness, the muscles in the front of the eye relax, causing the opening in the eye to enlarge. This hole in the eye is called the pupil, and it regulates the amount of light that enters the eye. In bright light, the opening starts to close, thus allowing only a small amount of light to enter the eye. This small hole not only protects the eye from bright light, but improves the image formed on the retina. A sharp image is produced when the extra light is shut out.

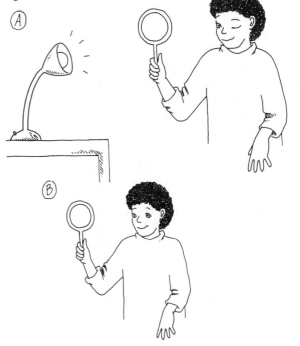

68. Eye Lens

Purpose To demonstrate how an eye lens works.

Materials magnifying lens   ruler
sheet of typing paper

Procedure
- Darken a room.
- Hold the magnifying lens about 5 feet (1½ m) from an open window.
- Position the paper on the opposite side of the lens from the window.
- Slowly move the paper back and forth from the lens until a clear image of the window and objects outside appear.

Results A small, colored, inverted image forms on the paper.

Why? Just like the light passing through the lens in a human eye, the light changes direction as it passes through. The light hits the paper in the same way that light hits the retina when it passes through the lens of an eye and forms an inverted image. Nerves on the retina send the message of the inverted image to the brain, which turns the image right side up again.

69. Finger Monocle

Purpose To make a monocle.

Materials newspaper

Procedure
- Roll one index finger in tightly to form a very tiny hole about the size of the point of a writing pen.
- Hold the newspaper close enough to your eyes so that the print is just barely blurred.
- Close one eye and with the open eye look through the hole made by your index finger at the blurred newsprint.

Results The words are less blurred and more readable.

Why? Squinting or looking through a small hole causes the eye lens to thicken. The light entering the thicker lens allows a sharper image to be formed on the retina of the eye.

---

70. Color Trickery

Purpose To demonstrate that it takes different lengths of time for the brain to record the presence of color waves.

Materials black marker
3 in. × 5 in. (7.6 cm × 12.7 cm) unlined index card
straight pin
pencil
ruler

Procedure
- Draw a circle with about a 2-in. (5 cm) diameter in the center of the index card.
- Reproduce the pattern from illustration A.
- Color the dark sections with the black ink marker.
- Push the straight pin through the center of the circle.
- Insert the point of the pin into the eraser of the pencil.
- Spin the card.
- Focus your eyes on a spot just past the rotating circle.

Results Various combinations of colors appear as the disk rotates. The colors change as the circle changes speed.

Why? Scientists are not sure exactly why the spinning patterns causes you to see colors. A current theory is that as the pattern of black and white spins, flashes of light due to the changes in color intensity are produced. These flashes act like a Morse-code signal telling the brain it sees a particular color for that particular code. The code and color seen change as the number of flashes increases or decreases with the speed of the rotating pattern.

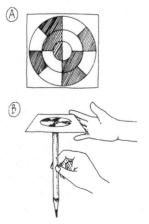

71. Water Drop Lens

Purpose A water drop is used to simulate an eye lens.

Materials one 6-in. (15 cm) piece of 20-gauge wire
pencil
bowl
newspaper

Procedure
- Twist one end of the wire around the pencil to make a round loop.
- Fill the bowl with water.
- Dip the wire into the water with the open loop pointing up.
- Lift the loop carefully out of the water and hold it over the newspaper. You want a large rounded drop of water to stay in the hole of the wire loop.
- Look through the water drop at the letters on the page. You may have to move the loop up and down to find a position that makes the letters clear.

Results The letters are enlarged. If the letters look smaller, dip the loop into the water again.

Why? The water drop is curved outward and acts like a convex lens. This type of lens is used as a magnifying lens and is the type of lens in eyes. Sometimes the water drop stretches so tightly between the wire that it curves downward, forming a concave lens. This type of lens causes the letters to look small.

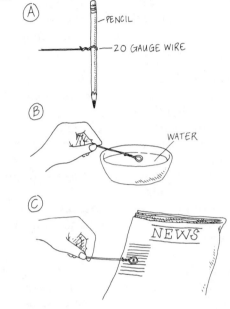

72. Hearing

Purpose To demonstrate how sound is heard.

Materials metal spoon   2 ft. (61 cm) of kite string

Procedure
- Tie the handle of the spoon in the center of the string.
- Wrap the ends of the string around both index fingers. Be sure that both strings are the same length.
- Place the tip of an index finger in each ear.
- Lean over so that the spoon hangs freely and tap it against the side of a table.

Results It sounds like a church bell.

Why? The metal in the spoon starts to vibrate when struck. These vibrations are transmitted up the string to the ears. The ability to hear is due to one's ability to detect vibrations. Objects must vibrate to produce a sound. The vibrating object causes the air around it to move. Vibrating air molecules enter the ear and strike the eardrum, causing it to vibrate. These vibrations continue to travel through bones and fluids in the ear until they reach a nerve that sends the message to the brain.

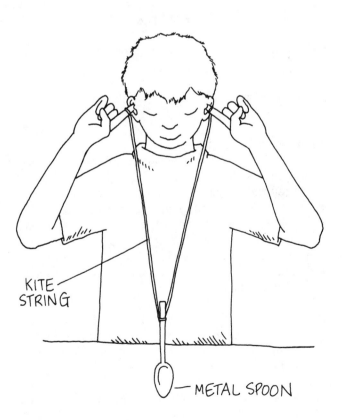

73. Soft Bones

Purpose To produce a flexible bone by removing minerals.

Materials 1 thin uncooked chicken bone such as a wingbone or wishbone
1 jar with a lid (jar must be large enough to hold the bone)
white vinegar

Procedure
- Ask an adult to clean the uncooked bone of all muscles and tendons.
- Allow the bone to dry overnight.
- Place the bone in the jar. Add enough vinegar to cover the bone.
- Secure the lid and allow the jar to stand undisturbed overnight.
- Remove the bone and rinse with water.
- Test the flexibility of the bone daily for 7 days by bending it back and forth with your fingers.

Results The ends of the bone become soft first. As time passes, the bone starts to soften toward the center. The final result is a soft, rubbery bone that can be twisted.

Why? Minerals in the bone cause it to be strong and rigid. The vinegar removes these minerals from the bone, leaving it soft and pliable.

74. Heartbeat

Purpose To observe the vibration of a match due to the pulsation of blood in the wrist.

Materials modeling clay   table
match

Procedure
- Insert the match into a very small piece of clay (the smaller the better).
- Flatten the bottom of the clay.
- Place your wrist, palm side up, on a table.
- Place the clay on your wrist, and move the clay around on the thumb side of the wrist until the match starts to slowly vibrate back and forth.
- Count the number of vibrations that the match makes in one minute.

Results The match vibrates back and forth with a regular beat. For adults it will vibrate 60 to 80 times in one minute. The vibration for children is from 80 to 140 beats per minute.

Why? As the heart contracts, blood is forced through the blood vessels. The blood moves at a rhythmic rate, causing the blood vessels in the wrist to pulsate. All blood vessels have this throbbing motion, but the vessels in the wrist are close to the surface of the skin and can be felt more easily. The movement of the blood under the clay causes it and the match to vibrate.

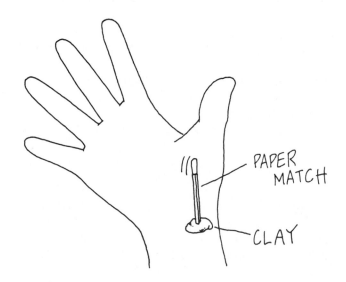

75. Skin Color

Purpose To observe the effect of light on skin color.

Materials Band-Aid

Procedure
- Place a Band-Aid around the end of one finger.
- Leave the bandage on for 2 days.
- Remove the bandage and observe the color of the skin over the entire finger.

Results The skin color is much lighter where it was covered by the bandage.

Why? Special cells in animals contain dark brown grains called melanin. In the absence of light, the grains group together, producing skin with a light appearance. Melanin responds to light by spreading out, causing the skin to be much darker. People with dark skin have more melanin. Albinos have no melanin in their skin. The skin of albinos is white.

76. Input-Output

Purpose To demonstrate that the output message from the brain is not always correct.

Materials a partner

Procedure
- Place the palm of your hand against the palm of your partner's hand.
- With the thumb and index finger of your free hand, rub the outside of the joined index fingers.

Results It feels as if part of your finger is asleep.

Why? The brain is like a computer, and it contains programs. When you rub your finger, both sides of the touched finger send messages to the brain. The finger doing the rubbing also sends messages. These messages are paired up and the resulting sensation is that you have rubbed both sides of your finger. There was a missing message when the fingers were joined with your partner's. This touching was the input message; the output message was that there is no feeling on one side of your finger. The brain takes in and feeds out information. Even though we know better, we cannot change the output.

77. Retainer

Purpose To demonstrate the overlapping of images in your mind.

Materials   white poster board   paper hole punch
marking pen   ruler
scissors   string

Procedure

- Draw and cut a circle with a 4 in. (10 cm) diameter from the poster board.
- Use the hole punch to make two holes on each side of the paper circle.
- Measure and cut two 24-in. (60-cm) pieces of string.
- Thread the string through the holes as shown in the diagram.
- Use the marker to draw a large empty fishbowl on one side of the paper circle, and a small fish on the opposite side.
- Hold the strings and twirl the paper disk around in a circle about 25 times to twist the strings.
- Pull the strings straight out with your fingers.
- Observe the spinning paper disk.

Results The fish appears to be inside the bowl.

Why? You see each picture as it passes in front of your eyes. Your eye retains the image of each picture for about 1/16 of a second. The image of the bowl is still being retained when the fish image is projected on the eye. This causes an overlapping of the pictures in your mind, and thus the fish appears to be inside the bowl.

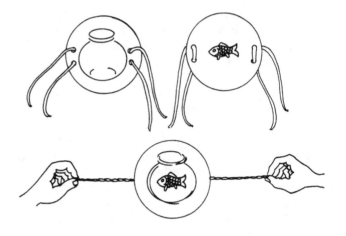

78. Winker

Purpose To demonstrate persistence of vision by making a *phenakistoscope* (a viewing device).

Materials   marking pen   pushpin
scissors   pencil
ruler   mirror
poster board—10 in.
(25 cm) square

Procedure

- Draw and cut a 10-in. (25-cm) diameter circle from a piece of poster board.
- On one side of the paper disk, use the pencil to divide the circle into 12 equal parts.
- At each of the 12 divisions, cut a slot about ¼ in. (.63 cm) wide and 1 in. (2.5 cm) deep.
- Draw faces on the unmarked side of the disk. On each of the 12 faces, change the position of the eyelid on one eye as in the diagram.
- Insert a pushpin through the center of the disk and into the eraser of a pencil. Spin the disk to hollow out the hole made by the pin so that it turns easily.
- While standing in front of a mirror, hold the end of the pencil so that the side with the faces points toward the mirror.

- Spin the paper as you look through the slots in the disk at the mirror.

Results The mirror image of the turning disk looks like a face with one eye blinking again and again.

Why? Looking through the slits allows you to see each face for only a fraction of a second until the rotating disk brings another drawing into view. Your brain holds on to each image for about 1/16 of a second, by which time the image of another face has spun into view. This is called *persistence of vision*. Because one eye's position is slightly changed in each drawing, the overlapping of the images of the face gives you the illusion that the eye on the faces is blinking.

79. ZZZZ'S

Purpose To determine what makes a person snore.

Materials wax paper   ruler
scissors

Procedure

- Measure and cut a 6-in. (15-cm) square of wax paper.
- Place your hands on the sides of the paper square.
- Hold the paper against your lips.
- Hum your favorite song.
- Hum the same song without the paper.

Results The song sounds natural without the paper, but with it you hear a strange vibrating tune. The wax paper also tickles your lips.

Why? Sound is produced by vibrating materials. Humming causes the wax paper to vibrate. Snoring, like all sounds, is nothing more than the vibration of soft tissue within the mouth. As you sleep, gravity pulls your tongue, *uvula* (the hanging piece of skin at the top of your throat), and other soft tissue in the mouth down, causing the airway to be partially blocked. As you inhale, air moves through the small passage and causes the soft parts of the mouth to vibrate. This vibrating sound is called snoring.

80. Around and Around

Purpose To produce the illusion of a spinning circle.

Materials index card   ruler
marker   pencil

Procedure

- Use a marker to make a dot on the edge of the card in the center of one of the long sides.
- Lay a ruler with its straight edge from the corner of the card to the dot as shown in the diagram.
- With the marker, make about 30 evenly spaced dots on the card along the straight edge of the ruler.
- Push the point of a pencil through the center of the card.
- Hold the pencil upright with one hand and spin the card with your free hand.
- Look at the spinning card.

Results A circle appears on the spinning card.

Why? What you see is an *illusion* (a false mental picture). Every spot on the line traces out a circle as the card is spun, but the spot closest to the pencil traces the slowest-moving circle. Your eye retains the image of this spot as it slowly moves around in its small circular path. This retention of vision gives you the illusion of a solid circular line instead of one spot.

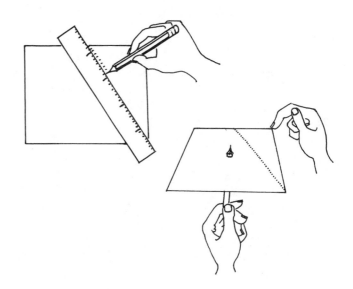

III
Chemistry

81. Kerplunk!

Purpose To demonstrate inertia, a property of matter.

Facts *Matter* can be defined as anything that takes up space and has inertia.

Inertia is a resistance to a change in motion or rest.

Materials index card   nickel
drinking glass

Procedure
- Lay the index card over the mouth of the glass.
- Place the coin on top of the card, centered over the mouth of the glass.
- Snap the card with your finger.

Results The card quickly moves forward and the coin drops into the glass.

Why? The stationary card and coin are said to be at rest. They remain motionless because of their inertia. *Inertia* is the tendency of a material not to

change its motion or state of rest. When the card is snapped, it slips under the stationary coin. *Gravity* pulls the coin down into the glass.

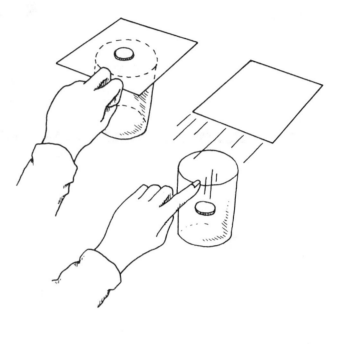

82. Paper Hop

Purpose To illustrate that atoms have positive and negative parts.

Materials piece of notebook paper
paper hole punch
table
balloon (use a size easily held in your hand)

Procedure
- Use the hole punch to cut 15 to 20 small circles from the piece of paper.
- Separate the circles and spread them on a table.
- Inflate the balloon and tie it.
- Rub the balloon against your hair, about five strokes. It is important that your hair be clean, dry, and free from oil.
- Hold the balloon close to, but not touching, the paper circles.

Results The paper circles will hop up and stick to the balloon.

Why? Paper is an example of matter, and all matter is made up of *atoms*. Each atom has a positive center

with negatively charged electrons spinning around the outside. The balloon rubs the electrons off the hair, giving the balloon an excess of negative charges. The positive part of the paper circles is attracted to the excessive negative charge on the balloon. This attraction between the positive and negative charge is great enough to overcome the force of gravity, and the circles will hop upward toward the balloon.

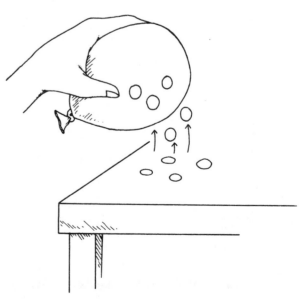

83. Unseen Movement

Purpose To observe the effect of molecular motion.

Materials dark food coloring
tall, one-half pint (250 ml) jar of water

Procedure
- Place the jar of water where it will not be moved or touched for 24 hours.
- Hold the food coloring container above the water and allow two drops of coloring to fall into the water.
- Observe immediately and then again in 24 hours.

Results The drops of coloring sink to the bottom of the jar, forming colored streaks in the water as they fall. After 24 hours, the water is evenly colored.

Why? The atoms and molecules that make up matter are all in constant motion. Though not seen by the naked eye, water molecules are moving. The small particles of food coloring are being pushed and shoved around by the moving water molecules. Given enough time, the colored particles will be evenly spread throughout the jar of vibrating water. The movement of the color throughout the water is called *diffusion*.

84. A Rising Ball

Purpose To observe the property that no two pieces of matter can occupy the same space at the same time.

Materials glass quart (liter) jar (large-mouthed with a lid)
uncooked rice
small jacks ball or walnut

Procedure
- Fill the quart jar one-quarter full with uncooked rice.
- Put the ball or walnut inside the jar and close the lid.
- Hold the jar upright then turn it over. *Note:* Add more rice if the ball cannot be covered by the rice.
- Shake the jar back and forth vigorously until the ball surfaces. **DO NOT SHAKE UP AND DOWN.**

Results The ball or walnut comes to the surface.

Why? There are spaces between the grains of rice. As the jar is shaken, the rice gets closer together. This is referred to as *settling*. As the rice moves together, it pushes the ball upward. Two pieces of matter cannot occupy the same space at the same time; thus the ball is moved by the packing together of the rice grains.

85. No Room

Purpose To try to inflate a balloon inside a bottle.

Materials cola bottle or any small-mouthed bottle
balloon
Note: The balloon must be large enough to fit over the mouth of the bottle.

Procedure
- Hold on to the top of the balloon and push the bottom inside the bottle.
- Stretch the top of the balloon over the mouth of the bottle.
- Try to inflate the balloon by blowing into it.

Results The balloon expands only slightly.

Why? The bottle is filled with air. Blowing into the balloon causes the air molecules inside the bottle to move closer together, but only slightly. The air is in the way of the balloon, thus preventing it from inflating.

86. Creeper

Purpose To demonstrate the cleaning of water by capillary action (rising of liquids in small tubes).

Materials 2 bowls, quart (liter) size
2 tbs. (30 ml) of dirt
2 connected sheets of paper toweling
tablespoon (15 ml)
cooking pot
table

Procedure
- Fill one of the bowls half full with water.
- Add 2 tablespoons (30 ml) dirt to the water; stir.
- Turn a cooking pot upside down on top of a table.
- Set the bowl of muddy water on top of the pot.
- Place the empty bowl next to the pot.
- Fold two connected sheets of paper toweling lengthwise three times to form a long strip.
- Place one end of the paper strip in the muddy water and let the other end hang down into the empty bowl.
- Allow the bowls to stand undisturbed for 24 hours.

Results Clear water moves out of the muddy water through the paper towel and into the empty bowl.

Caution: Do not drink the water because it may contain harmful bacteria.

Why? The spaces between the fibers in the paper are tiny, tubelike structures through which the water moves. By *capillary action,* the water clings and even slightly climbs the sides of the tubes through the paper. This produces a *concave* (curved down) surface to the water. However, water molecules pull on each other, and this pull causes the curved surface to contract, becoming flat and pulling up the middle. Again the water molecules climb the sides, producing a concave surface, and again they pull themselves into a flat surface. This continued process of climbing and pulling causes the water to creep up through the paper towel and over the edge, where *gravity* (the downward pull on an object toward the center of the earth) pulls the water down into the bowl. The dirt particles are left behind because they are too heavy to be carried up through the tubes.

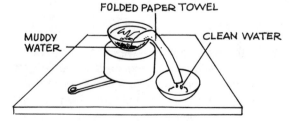

FOLDED PAPER TOWEL

MUDDY WATER

CLEAN WATER

87. Currents of Color

Purpose To demonstrate how a detergent can cause other molecules to move.

Materials milk
　　　　　saucer
　　　　　food coloring—red, blue, and green
　　　　　liquid dish detergent

Procedure
- Pour enough milk into a saucer to cover its bottom.
- Add two drops of each food coloring, red, blue, and green. Space these drops around the surface of the milk.
- Hold the detergent bottle over the center of the saucer and squeeze one drop of detergent out of the bottle.
- Observe the movement of the colors.

Results Currents of color quickly move out in all directions from the center of the dish. Swirling movements of separate colors are seen across the surface of the milk during the first two minutes. Within the next one to two minutes, the moving colors begin to mix together and finally form a grey mixture.

Why? The drops of colors temporarily remain separate because of the drops of fat in the milk. These fatty drops do not mix well with the watery food coloring, and thus the colors are kept separate. The colors move outward because surface water molecules pull on the molecules of color with equal force in all directions. Placing the soap in the center weakened the pull of the water molecules in the center, and the stronger-clinging water molecules on the opposite side of the color molecules pulled them across the surface of the water toward the edge of the saucer. As the drops of fat are broken into smaller particles by the detergent, they spread out, allowing more of the food coloring and milk to mix.

88. No Heat

Purpose To make water appear to boil with only the touch from a finger.

Materials cotton handkerchief
　　　　　clear drinking glass (with straight,
　　　　　　　smooth sides)
　　　　　rubber band

Procedure
- Wet the handkerchief with water. Squeeze out any excess water.
- Fill the glass to the top with water.
- Drape the wet cloth over the mouth of the glass.
- Place the rubber band over the cloth in the middle of the glass to hold the cloth close to the glass.
- Use your fingers to push the cloth down about 1 inch (2-3 cm) below the water level.
- Pick the glass up, hold the bottom with one hand, and turn it upside down. *Note:* There will be some spillage, so do this over a sink.
- Place the other hand under the hanging cloth and hold the glass. At this point, one hand is holding the cloth next to the glass with the free end of the cloth draped over this hand.
- With the free hand, push down on the bottom of the glass. Allow the glass to slowly slip down into the cloth.

Results The water does not fall out of the glass, and it appears to start boiling.

Why? Water does not flow out of the cloth because the tiny holes in the cloth are filled with water. Water molecules have a strong attraction for each other that draws them close together. This causes the water to behave as if a thin skin were covering each hole in the cloth, preventing the water in the glass from falling out.
　　Pushing the glass down causes the cloth to be pulled out of the glass. This outward movement of the cloth creates a vacuum inside and the air outside is pushed through the cloth. Small bubbles of air form inside the water, giving an appearance of boiling water.

89. Floating Sticks

Purpose To observe the pulling power of water molecules.

Materials 3 toothpicks quart (liter) glass bowl
liquid dish soap

Procedure
- Fill the bowl three-quarters full with water.
- Place two toothpicks side by side on the surface in the center of the water.
- Treat the third toothpick by dipping its point in liquid detergent. *Note:* Only a very small amount of detergent is needed.
- Touch the treated toothpick tip between the floating sticks.

Results The sticks *quickly* move away from each other.

Why? The surface of water acts as if a thin skin were stretched across it. This allows objects to float on top. Detergent breaks the attraction between the molecules where it touches, causing the water molecules to move outward and taking the floating sticks with them. This outward movement occurs because the water molecules are pulling on each other. It is almost as if the molecules were all playing tug of war, and any break causes the "tuggers" to fall backward.

90. Moving Drop

Purpose To demonstrate the attractive force between water molecules.

Materials 1-foot (30-cm) sheet of wax paper
toothpick
eyedropper
water

Procedure
- Spread the wax paper on a table.
- Use the eyedropper to position three or four separate small drops of water on the paper.
- Wet the toothpick with water.
- Bring the tip of the wet pick near, but not touching, one of the water drops. Repeat with the other drops.

Results The drop moves toward the toothpick.

Why? Water molecules have an attraction for each other. This attraction is strong enough to cause the water drop to move toward the water on the toothpick. The attraction of the water molecules for each other is due to the fact that each molecule has a positive and a negative side. The positive side of one molecule attracts the negative side of another molecule.

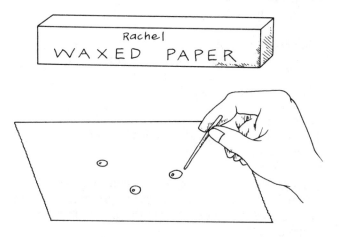

91. Soap Bubbles

Purpose To make a soap bubble solution and to blow soap bubbles.

Materials liquid dish soap
cup (250 ml)
8-in. (20-cm) piece of 20-gauge wire; any thin bendable wire will work

Procedure
- Fill the cup one-half full with the dish soap.
- Add enough water to fill the cup. Stir.
- Make a 2-in. (5-cm) diameter loop in one end of the wire.
- Dip the loop into the soap solution.
- Hold the loop, with the thin layer of soap stretched across it, about four inches from your mouth.
- Gently blow through the film of soap.

Results Bubbles of soap should be produced. If the soap film breaks, try blowing more gently. Add 1 tablespoon (15 ml) of soap to the solution if the bubbles continue to break. More soap should be added until bubbles are produced.

Why? The soap and water molecules link together

to form a zig-zag pattern. This irregular pattern allows the thin layer of liquid to stretch outward when blown into.

92. Foamy Soda

Purpose To observe gas bubbles being pushed out of a soda by particles of salt.

Materials small baby-food jar
soda, any flavor carbonated beverage
1 tsp (5 ml) table salt

Procedure
- Fill the jar one-half full with the soda.
- Add 1 teaspoon (5 ml) of salt to the soda.

Results Bubbles form in the liquid, then foam appears on top of the soda.

Why? Each bubble seen in the soda is a collection of carbon dioxide gas. Salt and carbon dioxide are both examples of matter and matter takes up space. When the salt is added to the cola, bubbles of carbon dioxide stick to the grains. Larger bubbles form and rise to the top, bringing small amounts of soda with them. This movement of the gas forms the foam on top of the liquid, and the process is called effervescence.

93. Erupting Volcano

Purpose To simulate a volcanic eruption.

Materials soda bottle   1 tbs. (15 ml) baking soda
               baking pan   1 cup (250 ml) vinegar
               dirt   red food coloring

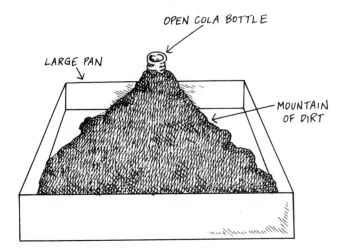

Procedure
- Place the soda bottle in the pan.
- Shape moist dirt around the bottle to form a mountain. Do not cover the bottle's mouth and do not get dirt inside the bottle.
- Pour 1 tablespoon (15 ml) of baking soda into the bottle.
- Color 1 cup (250 ml) of vinegar with the red food coloring, and pour the liquid into the bottle.

Results Red foam sprays out the top and down the mountain of dirt.

Why? The baking soda reacts with the vinegar to produce carbon dioxide gas. The gas builds up enough pressure to force the liquid out the top of the bottle. The mixture of the gas and the liquid produces the foam.

94. How Long?

Purpose To time the release of bubbles produced by one Alka-Seltzer tablet.

Materials soda bottle
               measuring cup (250 ml)
               clay ball, the size of a walnut
               18-in. (45-cm) piece of aquarium tubing
               1 Alka-Seltzer tablet

Procedure
- Pour 1/4 cup (60 ml) of water into the soda bottle.
- Squeeze the clay around the tubing about 2 inches (5 cm) from one end.
- Fill the jar with water.
- Place the free end of the tube in the jar of water.
- Break the Alka-Seltzer tablet into small pieces; quickly drop the pieces into the soda bottle.
- Immediately insert the tube into the bottle; seal the opening with the clay.
- Record the time.
- Watch and record the time when the bubbling stops.

Results The tablet immediately reacts with the water to produce bubbles. The bubbles are released for about 25 minutes.

Why? The dry acid and baking soda in the tablet are able to combine with the water to form carbon dioxide gas. It is the carbon dioxide gas that moves through the tube and forms bubbles in the glass of water. The bubbling stops when all the material has reacted.

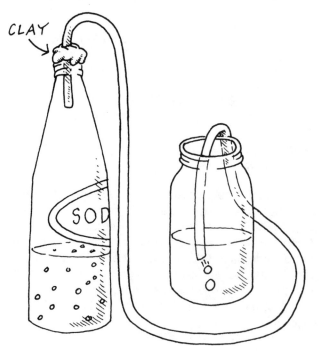

95. Browning Apple

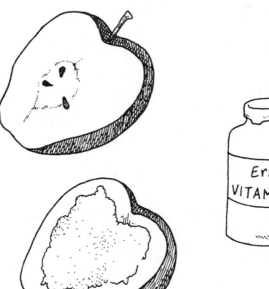

Purpose An investigation of the effect that oxygen has on the darkening of fruit.

Materials apple   vitamin C tablet

Procedure
- Cut the unpeeled apple in half.
- Crush the vitamin C tablet and sprinkle the powder over the cut surface of one of the apple halves.
- Allow both apple sections to sit uncovered for one hour.
- Observe the color of each section.

Results The untreated section turns brown, but the section treated with vitamin C is unchanged.

Why? Apples and other fruit, such as pears and bananas, discolor when bruised or peeled and exposed to air. This discoloration is caused by chemicals called *enzymes*. The enzymes are released by the damaged cells and react with oxygen to digest the cells of the fruit. Rapid color and taste changes occur because of the reaction with oxygen. Vitamin C prevents the darkening by reacting with the enzyme before it can start digesting the cell tissue.

96. Aging Paper

Purpose To observe the rapid aging of a newspaper.

Materials newspaper   automobile

Procedure
- Lay a piece of newspaper in an automobile so that the sun's rays hit it.
- Leave the paper in the car for 5 days.

Results The newspaper appears to have rapidly aged. It changes from white to yellow in color.

Why? This reaction is unique because it is the reverse of most reactions with oxygen. Usually the addition of oxygen causes the color to become lighter. The materials used to make the newspaper are yellow in color. The chemicals added to turn the paper white do so by removing oxygen. Placing the paper in the car allows the sunlight to heat up the air and the paper, causing oxygen to combine with the chemicals in the paper. The addition of the oxygen changes the paper back to its original yellow color. All newspaper will turn yellow after a period of time. The sun's light just speeded up the aging process.

97. Stick On

Purpose To demonstrate how air is cleaned by adsorbent chemicals.

Materials 1 cup (250 ml)   marking pen
              baking soda   adult helper
              shoe box with a lid 1 onion
              measuring tablespoon saucer
                (15 ml)
              2 pint-size Ziploc® bags

Procedure

- Pour 1 cup (250 ml) of baking soda into a shoe box.
- Remove one tablespoon (15 ml) of baking soda from the box and place it in a Ziploc® bag. With the marking pen, label the bag "UNUSED."
- Evenly spread the rest of baking soda over the bottom of the box.
- Ask an adult helper to peel an onion and cut it in four parts.
- Place the pieces of onion in a saucer.
- Set the saucer of onions inside the shoe box.
- Place the lid on the box.
- After 24 hours, remove a tablespoon (15 ml) of the baking soda and place it in a Ziploc® bag. Label the bag "USED."

- Open the bags one at a time and smell the contents.

Results The contents of the bag marked "USED" smell like an onion.

Why? Baking soda is *adsorbent* (other chemicals stick to its surface). Being adsorbent is different from being *absorbent*. A sponge absorbs or picks up water by taking the water into the material of the sponge. When the baking soda adsorbs the gases given off by the cut onion, the gas molecules stick to the surface of the baking soda. The more the baking soda is spread out, the greater is its surface area and the more adsorbing it is. Baking soda is often placed inside refrigerators to adsorb odors.

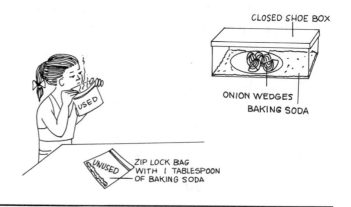

CLOSED SHOE BOX

ONION WEDGES

BAKING SODA

USED

UNUSED   ZIP LOCK BAG
          WITH 1 TABLESPOON
          OF BAKING SODA

---

98. Holes

Purpose To determine why there are holes in bread slices.

Materials 1 bowl, 1 qt. (1 liter)
              measuring cup (250 ml)
              1 cup (250 ml) flour
              measuring tablespoon (15 ml)
              3 tablespoons (45 ml) sugar
              1 package yeast, ¼ oz. (7 g)
              stirring spoon
              1 bowl, 2 qt. (2 liter)
              1 paper towel

Procedure

- In a 1-quart (1-liter) bowl mix together 1 cup (250 ml) of flour, 3 tablespoons (45 ml) of sugar, 1 package of yeast, and 1 cup (250 ml) of warm water from the faucet. Stir.
- Into the empty 2-quart (2-liter) bowl pour 3 cups (750 ml) of warm water from the faucet.
- Set the small bowl with the flour mixture into the larger bowl of warm water.
- Cover the top of the bowls with the paper towel.
- Lift the paper towel every 30 minutes for 4 hours and observe the surface of the mixture in the bowl.

Results A few bubbles appear on the surface of the mixture after 30 minutes. As time passes, more bubbles are seen and the surface of the mixture rises in the bowl.

Why? Making bread involves a *chemical reaction* (the changing to new substances). One of the ingredients in making bread is a tiny, one-celled living fungus called yeast. This hungry plant eats the sugar and changes it into carbon dioxide gas, alcohol, and energy. The bubbles observed in this experiment are carbon dioxide; they produce holes as they rise through the flour mixture. This same gas causes bread to rise during baking as the bubbles push the dough outward. Holes made by pockets of gas can be seen in slices of baked bread.

99. Glob

Purpose To discover how a non-Newtonian fluid behaves.

Materials 4-oz. (120-ml) bottle of white school glue
         1 pint (500 ml) jar
         food coloring, any color
         1 bowl, 2 qt. (liter)
         measuring cup (250 ml)
         1 pint (500 ml) distilled water
         1 teaspoon (5 ml) borax powder (found in the supermarket with laundry detergents)
         measuring teaspoon (5 ml)
         stirring spoon

Procedure
- Pour the glue into a pint (500 ml) jar.
- Fill the empty glue bottle with distilled water and pour the water into the jar containing the glue. Add 10 drops of food coloring and stir well.
- Put 1 cup (250 ml) distilled water and 1 teaspoon (5 ml) borax powder into the bowl. Stir until the powder dissolves.
- Slowly pour the colored glue into the bowl containing the borax. Stir as you pour.

- Take the thick glob that forms out of the bowl. Knead the glob with your hands until it is smooth and dry.
- Try these experiments with the glob:
  - Roll it into a ball and bounce it on a smooth surface.
  - Hold it in your hands and quickly pull the ends in opposite directions.
  - Hold it in your hands and slowly pull the ends in opposite directions.

Results Kneading quickly dries the glob and results in a piece of soft pliable material that bounces slightly when dropped. It snaps if pulled quickly, but stretches if pulled slowly.

Why? This most unusual material is an example of a *non-Newtonian fluid*. *Fluids* (anything that can flow) have a property called *viscosity* (the thickness of a fluid or its resistance to flowing). In the 1600s, Sir Isaac Newton stated that only a change in temperature could change the viscosity of a fluid. Fluids that change viscosity due to temperature changes are called Newtonian fluids. Non-Newtonian fluids' ability to flow, however, can also be changed by applying a force. Pushing or pulling on the piece of glob makes it thicker and less able to flow.

100. Green Pennies

Purpose To give pennies a green coating.

Materials paper towel   vinegar
           saucer   3–5 pennies

Procedure
- Fold the paper towel in half; fold again to form a square.
- Place the folded towel in the saucer.
- Pour enough vinegar into the saucer to wet the towel.
- Place the pennies on top of the wet paper towel.
- Wait 24 hours.

Results The tops of the pennies are green.

Why? Vinegar's chemical name is acetic acid. The acetate part of the acid combines with the copper on the pennies to form copper acetate, the green coating you see on the pennies.

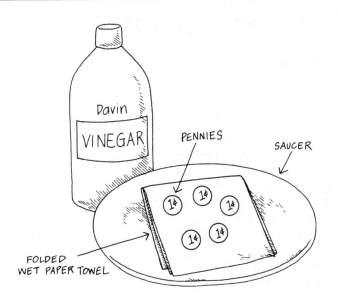

101. Breakdown

Purpose To change hydrogen peroxide into water and oxygen with the aid of a potato.

Materials hydrogen peroxide
raw potato
5-oz. (150-ml) paper cup

Procedure
- Fill the paper cup one-half full with hydrogen peroxide.
- Add a slice of raw potato to the cup.
- Observe the results. Look specifically for bubbles of gas.

Results Bubbles of gas are given off.

Why? Raw potatoes contain the enzyme *catalase*. Enzymes are chemicals found in living cells. Their purpose is to speed up the breakdown of complex food chemicals into smaller, simpler, more usable parts. Catalase from the potato's cells causes the hydrogen peroxide to quickly break apart into water and oxygen gas.

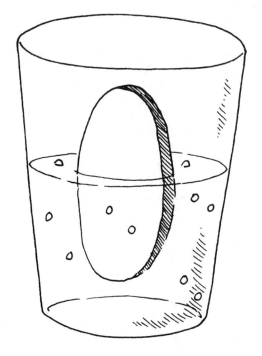

102. Starch I.D.

Purpose To determine how to test materials for the presence of starch.

Materials 1/4 teaspoon (1 ml) flour
measuring tablespoon (45 ml)
saucer
tincture of iodine

Procedure
- Place 1/4 teaspoon (1 ml) of flour in a saucer.
- Add 3 tablespoons (45 ml) of water and stir.
- Add three or four drops of the tincture of iodine.

Results The combination of starch and iodine produces an intense blue-purple color.

Why? Starch is a very large chemical molecule. It looks like a long, twisted chain with many branches sticking out. This long, twisted chain is thought to capture the iodine inside its spiral pattern. The spiral of starch with iodine caught on the inside produces the color.

103. Magic Writing

Purpose To write a message that magically appears.

Materials soup bowl
cup (250 ml)
tincture of iodine
eyedropper
lemon
notebook paper
art brush

Procedure
- Pour ½ cup (125 ml) water into a soup bowl.
- Add 10 drops of tincture of iodine to the water and stir.
- Squeeze the juice of the lemon into the cup.
- Cut a section from the notebook paper. The paper must fit inside the bowl.
- Dip the art brush into the lemon juice and write a message on the piece of paper.
- Allow the juice to dry on the paper.
- Submerse the paper in the iodine solution in the bowl.

Results The paper turns a blue-purple except where the message was written. The words are outlined by the dark background.

Why? The starch in the paper combines with the iodine to form iodine-starch molecules. These molecules are blue-purple in color. Vitamin C combines with iodine to form a colorless molecule. The area covered with lemon juice remains unchanged because the paper is coated with vitamin C from the lemon.

104. Curds and Whey

Purpose To separate milk into its solid and liquid parts.

Materials milk
vinegar
small baby food jar
measuring tablespoon (15 ml)

Procedure
- Fill the jar with fresh milk.
- Add 2 tablespoons (30 ml) of vinegar and stir.
- Allow the jar to sit for two to three minutes.

Results The milk separates into two parts: a white solid and a clear liquid.

Why? A *colloid* is a mixture of liquids and very tiny particles that are spread throughout the liquid. Milk is an example of a colloid. The solid particles in milk are evenly spread throughout the liquid. Vinegar causes the small undissolved particles to clump together, forming a solid called *curd.* The liquid portion is referred to as *whey.*

105. Cooler

Purpose To demonstrate that evaporation takes away heat.

Materials clay flowerpot
bucket, large enough to hold the clay flowerpot
bowl, large enough to set the clay flowerpot in
table
two thermometers
2 drinking glasses, large enough to hold a thermometer
electric fan

Procedure
- Place the clay flowerpot in a bucket of water and let it soak for one day.
- Fill a bowl with water to a depth of about 1 in. (2.5 cm) and set the bowl on a table.
- Stand a thermometer in a glass and set the glass in the center of the bowl.
- Turn the wet flowerpot upside down and stand it in the bowl so that it covers the glass and the thermometer. Put a clay plug in the hole in the flowerpot.
- Stand a thermometer in a second glass, and set the glass on the table next to the bowl.
- Record the reading on both thermometers.
- Position a fan so that it blows equally on the flowerpot and on the glass standing on the table.
- Record the reading on both thermometers every 10 minutes for 1 hour. *Note:* Quickly replace the pot after each reading.

Results The temperature under the pot is lower than the temperature outside the pot.

Why? *Evaporation* occurs when a liquid absorbs enough heat energy to change from a liquid to a gas. As the water evaporates from the clay pot, it takes energy away; thus, the air underneath the pot is cooler than the air outside. Water from the bowl is soaked up by the pot, and so the evaporation and cooling process continues.

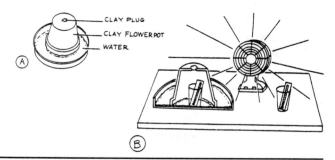

106. Frozen Orange Cubes

Purpose To determine whether orange juice will freeze like water.

Materials orange juice   refrigerator
ice tray

Procedure
- Fill half of the ice tray with orange juice.
- Fill the remaining half of the ice tray with water.
- Set the tray in the freezer overnight.
- Remove the frozen cubes.
- Carefully try to bite into a cube of orange juice and a cube of water.

Results The liquid orange juice and water both change to solids. The frozen cube of orange juice is not as firm as the cube of ice. It is easy to eat the cube of orange juice.

Why? The liquids both lost energy and changed from liquids to solids. The orange juice does not become as firm as the water because all the materials in the juice are not frozen. Many liquids freeze at a lower temperature than water does. Most of the frozen material in the juice is water. The juice cube is a combination of frozen and unfrozen material that makes it easy to eat.

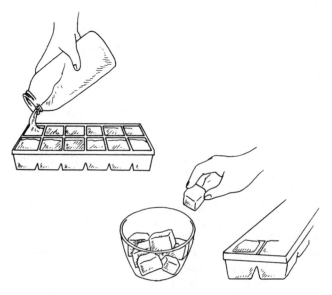

107. Crystal Ink

Purpose To produce a message written with shiny crystals.

Materials table salt
measuring teaspoon (5 ml)
measuring cup (250 ml)
stove with an oven
art brush
1 sheet black construction paper

Warning: Adult supervision is needed for use of the oven.

Procedure
- Add 3 teaspoons (15 ml) of salt to ¼ cup (60 ml) water.
- Ask an adult helper to warm the oven to 150°F (66°C).
- Use an art brush to write a message on the black paper. Stir the salt solution with the brush before making each letter. It is important to do this in order to produce a clear message.
- Have the adult helper turn the oven off and place the paper in the oven on top of the wire racks.
- Allow the paper to heat for 5 minutes or until it dries.

Results The message appears as white, shiny crystals on a black background.

Why? The water evaporates, leaving dry salt crystals on the paper. Evaporation is the process by which a material changes from a liquid to a gas. Liquid molecules are in constant motion, moving at different speeds and in different directions. When the molecules reach the surface with enough speed, they break through and become gas molecules. Heating the paper speeds up the evaporation process.

108. Fluffy and White

Purpose To observe the growth of fluffy white crystals.

Materials 4–5 charcoal briquets
2-qt. (2-liter) glass bowl
cup
1 tablespoon (15 ml) household ammonia
2 tablespoons (30 ml) water
1 tablespoon (15 ml) table salt
2 tablespoons (30 ml) laundry bluing

Procedure
- Place the charcoal briquets in the bowl.
- In a cup, mix together the ammonia, water, table salt, and bluing.
- Pour the liquid mixture over the charcoal.
- Allow the bowl to sit undisturbed for 72 hours.

Results White fluffy crystals form on top of the charcoal, and some climb up the sides of the bowl.

Why? There are different kinds of chemicals dissolved in the water. As the water evaporates, a thin layer of crystals forms on the surface. These crystals are porous like a sponge, and the liquid below moves into the openings. Water again evaporates at the surface, leaving another layer of crystals. This continues, resulting in a buildup of fluffy white crystals.

109. Escape

Purpose To demonstrate the removal of gas from a solution.

Materials   bottle of soda, 16 oz. (480 ml)
balloon, 9 in. (23 cm)
duct tape

Procedure
Note: This experiment should be performed outdoors.
■ Remove the cap from a bottle of soda.
■ Stretch the mouth of a balloon over the mouth of the soda bottle.
■ Use a strip of duct tape to secure the mouth of the balloon to the bottle.
■ Hold your thumb over the mouth of the bottle and shake the bottle gently.
■ Set the bottle down.
■ Observe the balloon and the contents of the bottle.

Results Bubbles form inside the bottle, and the balloon inflates.

Why? A *solution* is the combination of a solute and a solvent. A *solute* is a material being dissolved and

the *solvent* is a material doing the dissolving. In the soda, many solutes such as sugar, coloring, flavoring, and carbon dioxide are dissolved in the solvent, water. Large amounts of carbon dioxide are dissolved in the water by applying pressure. A "pop" is often heard when a bottle of soda is opened. Opening the bottle releases the pressure, and undissolved gas at the top of the bottle escapes so quickly that a sound is heard. Shaking the bottle causes more gas to leave the liquid, forming bubbles that can be seen as they rise to the surface. The escaping carbon dioxide applies enough pressure on the walls of the balloon to inflate it.

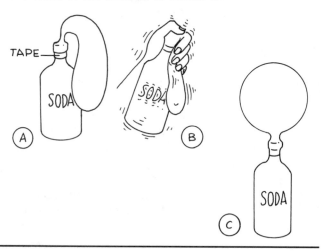

110. Erupting Colors

Purpose To produce erupting color bubbles.

Materials   clear glass bowl, 2 qt. (liter)
measuring tablespoon (15 ml)
liquid cooking oil
food coloring—red, blue, green
cup (250 ml)
fork

Procedure
■ Fill the bowl with water.
■ Pour 1 tablespoon of cooking oil into the cup.
■ Add 4 drops of each of the food coloring colors.
■ Use the fork to beat the oil and colors until thoroughly mixed.
■ Pour the mixture of oil and food colors onto the water in the bowl.
■ Observe the surface and side of the bowl for 5 to 10 minutes.

Results Small pools of oil spotted with tiny spheres of color float on the surface of the water. Individual spheres of color appear to explode outward, producing flat circles of color on the surface of the water with streams of color that sink down through the water.

Why? Oil and water are immiscible. *Immiscible* means they do not mix and will separate into layers. Because the food coloring is *water based* (it dissolves in water but not in oil), it remains in tiny spheres throughout the oil on the water's surface. The round, colored spheres sink through the oil layer and dissolve in the water layer below. At the moment the tiny drops of color touch the water, they quickly flatten on the surface, and long streamers of color begin their descent.

111. Tasty Solution

Purpose To determine the fastest way to dissolve candy.

Materials 3 bite-sized pieces of soft candy

Procedure
- Place one of the candy pieces in your mouth. *DO NOT* chew, and *DO NOT* move your tongue around.
- Record the time it takes for this candy piece to dissolve.
- Place a second candy piece in your mouth. *DO* move the candy back and forth with your tongue, but *DO NOT* chew.
- Record the time it takes to dissolve this candy piece.
- Place the third piece of candy in your mouth. *DO* move the candy back and forth with your tongue as you chew.
- Record the time it takes to dissolve this third piece of candy.

Results Moving the candy around and chewing it decrease the time necessary for dissolving.

Why? The candy dissolves in the saliva in your mouth to form a liquid solution. Solutions contain two parts, a solute and a solvent. The solvent is the saliva and the solute is the candy. The solute dissolves by spreading out evenly throughout the solvent. The candy can quickly dissolve when it is crushed by chewing and stirred by moving it around with the tongue.

112. Rainbow Effect

Purpose To observe the separation of colors in ink.

Materials coffee filter   paper clip
    green and black   saucer
        water-soluble pens

Procedure
- Fold the coffee filter in half.
- Fold it in half again.
- Make a dark green mark about 1 inch (2–3 cm) from the rounded edge of the folded filter.
- Make a second mark with the black marker about 1 inch (2–3 cm) from the rounded edge. The two marks are not to touch each other, but need to be on the same side.
- Secure the edge of the filter with the paper clip so that a cone is formed.
- Fill the saucer with water.
- Place the rounded edge of the cone in the water.
- Allow the paper to stand undisturbed for 1 hour.

Results It takes about 1 hour for the colors to separate. A trail of blue, yellow, and red is seen from the black mark, and the green mark produces a trail of blue and yellow.

Why? Black and green are combinations of other colors. As the water rises in the paper, the ink dissolves in it. Some of the colors rise to different heights, depending on the solubility of the chemicals producing the color. The more soluble chemicals move with the water to the top of the paper.

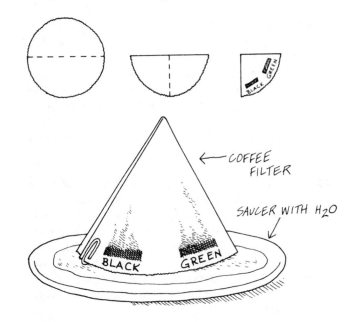

113. Immiscible

Purpose To observe the separation of an emulsion.

Materials ½ cup (125 ml) water
1-quart (1-liter) glass jar with a lid
blue food coloring
¼ cup (60 ml) liquid oil
measuring cup (250 ml)

Procedure
- Pour the water into the jar.
- Add 5 drops of the food coloring and stir.
- Slowly add the liquid oil.
- Secure the lid and shake the jar vigorously 10 times.
- Put the jar on a table and observe what happens.

Results At first it appears that the liquids have dissolved, but in only seconds three layers start to form. In only minutes, two layers are present. Liquid bubbles are present in all the layers.

Why? Oil and water are *immiscible,* meaning they do not mix. A combination of immiscible liquids is called an *emulsion.* Shaking the jar causes the oil and water to be mixed together, but they immediately start to separate. The heavier water sinks to the bottom, carrying with it trapped bubbles of oil. The center layer has an even distribution of oil and water, making it heavier than the oil but lighter than water. The top layer is mostly oil with trapped bubbles of water in it. It takes about eight hours for all the oil to rise and all the water to sink. Since only the water is colored, the food coloring has to be water soluble.

114. Clicking Coin

Purpose To observe the effects of expanding gas.

Materials 2-liter soda bottle   cup of water
quarter

Procedure
- Place the empty, uncapped soda bottle in the freezer for 5 minutes.
- Remove the bottle from the freezer and immediately cover the mouth with the wet coin. Wet the quarter by dipping the coin in the cup of water.

Results Within seconds, the coin starts to make a clicking sound as it rises and falls.

Why? Cooling causes matter to contract. The air in the bottle contracts and takes up less space. This allows more cold air to flow into the bottle. When it is removed from the freezer, this cold air starts to heat up and expand. The gas exerts enough pressure on the coin to cause it to rise on one side. The coin falls when the excess gas escapes. This process continues until the temperature inside the bottle equals that outside.
  Note: The coin will also stop clicking if it falls into a position that leaves a space for the gas to escape through. Try repositioning the coin.

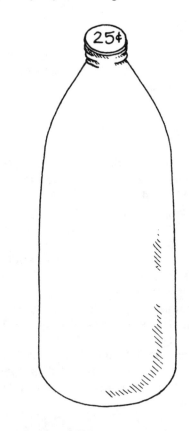

115. Chemical Heating

Purpose To show that a chemical reaction can produce heat.

Materials cooking or outdoor thermometer
        1 jar with lid (The thermometer must fit inside the closed jar.)
        1 steel wool pad without soap
        ¼ cup (60 ml) vinegar
        measuring cup (250 ml)

Procedure
- Place the thermometer inside the jar and close the lid. Record the temperature after 5 minutes.
- Soak one half of the steel wool pad in vinegar for 1 or 2 minutes.
- Squeeze out any excess liquid from the steel wool and wrap it around the bulb of the thermometer.
- Place the thermometer and the steel wool inside the jar. Close the lid.
- Record the temperature after 5 minutes.

Results The temperature rises.

Why? The vinegar removes any protective coating from the steel wool, allowing the iron in the steel to

rust. Rusting is a slow combination of iron with oxygen, and heat energy is always released. The heat released by the rusting of the iron causes the liquid in the thermometer to expand and rise in the thermometer tube.

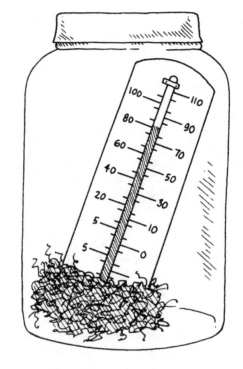

116. Radiation

Purpose To observe the effect that color has on the amount of radiation that an object absorbs.

Materials black construction paper   aluminum foil
    2 outdoor thermometers   100-watt light source
    stapler   ruler

Procedure
- Fold the black construction paper over one thermometer as shown and staple the sides.
- Fold a piece of aluminum foil over the second thermometer. Fold the sides of the foil as shown to secure them.
- Record the temperature on both thermometers.
- Place the light source about 1 foot (30 cm) above the pouches with the thermometers.
- Turn the light on and observe the temperature readings for 10 minutes.

Results The temperature reading is higher on the thermometer in the black pouch.

Why? Black objects absorb all the light waves.

Since none of the waves of light are reflected back to the viewer, the object looks black. This absorption of the waves of energy causes the object's temperature to rise. The aluminum foil does not absorb very many of the light waves, and thus its temperature is lower. Spring and summer clothes are usually light in color so the wearer stays cooler.

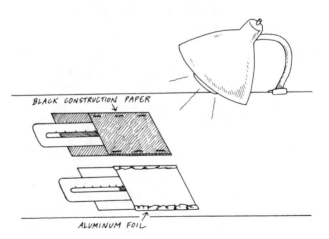

BLACK CONSTRUCTION PAPER

ALUMINUM FOIL

117. Cabbage Indicator

Purpose To make a solution that will indicate the presence of an acid or a base.

Materials 2 glass quart (liter) jars with lids
uncooked red cabbage
1 quart (liter) of distilled water
tea strainer
adult helper

Procedure
- Fill one jar with cabbage leaves that have been torn into small pieces.
- Ask your adult helper to heat the distilled water to boiling, and fill the jar containing the pieces of cabbage with the hot water.
- Allow the jar to stand until the water cools to room temperature.
- Pour the cooled cabbage solution through a tea strainer into the second quart (liter) jar. Discard the cabbage leaves.
- Store the cabbage juice in a refrigerator until needed.

Results After standing, the water covering the cabbage leaves turns blue.

Why? The hot water dissolves the colored chemicals in the cabbage. These colored chemicals turn red when mixed with an acid, and a base will produce a green color. Cabbage juice can be used to test for the presence of two different kinds of chemicals, *acid* and *base*.

118. Drinkable Acid

Purpose To identify a drinkable acid.

Materials cabbage indicator (prepared in Experiment 117)
glass
measuring tablespoon (15 ml)
lemonade

Procedure
- Place 1 tablespoon (15 ml) of cabbage indicator juice in the glass.
- Add 1 tablespoon (15 ml) of water.
- Add 1 tablespoon (15 ml) of lemonade and stir.

Results The blue indicator solution turns red.

Why? Lemonade, like the juice of all citrus fruits, contains citric acid. The blue cabbage solution turns red when mixed with an acid.

119. Turmeric Paper

Purpose To make a testing paper that will indicate the presence of a base.

Materials measuring cup (250 ml)
⅓ cup (80 ml) alcohol
measuring teaspoon (5 ml)
measuring spoon, ¼ teaspoon (1 ml)
turmeric powder
quart (liter) bowl
coffee filters
cookie sheet
Ziploc® plastic bag

Procedure

- Fill a measuring cup one-third full with alcohol.
- Stir ¼ teaspoon (1 ml) turmeric powder into the alcohol.
- Pour the solution into the quart bowl.
- Dip one coffee filter at a time in the turmeric solution.
- Place each wet filter on the cookie sheet and allow them to dry.
- Cut the dry papers into strips about ½ inch by 3 inches (1 cm by 7 cm).

- Store the strips in a Ziploc® plastic bag.

Results The dry turmeric paper is a bright yellow.

Why? *Indicators* are materials that have a specific color change. Turmeric is an indicator for a base. The color change is from yellow to red.

120. Wet Only

Purpose To observe that dry solids must be wet to be tested with turmeric paper.

Materials turmeric testing paper (prepared in Experiment 119)
baking soda
cup
measuring spoon, ½ tsp (2.5 ml)

Procedure

- Place ½ teaspoon (2.5 ml) of baking soda in the cup.
- Touch the dry powder with a dry piece of turmeric paper.
- Wet one end of the turmeric paper, touch the baking soda with the wet end.

Results There is no change when the dry paper is used. The wet paper turns red.

Why? Baking soda is basic, but it must be dissolved in water before it can react with the colored chemicals on the turmeric paper. The water allows the chemicals to mix together.

IV
Earth Science

121. Bulging Ball

Purpose To determine why the earth bulges at the equator.

Materials construction paper—
16 in. (40 cm) long
scissors
paper glue
paper hole punch
ruler
pencil

Procedure
- Measure and cut 2 separate strips, 1¼ in. × 16 in. (3 cm × 40 cm), from construction paper.
- Cross the strips at their centers and glue.
- Bring the four ends together, overlap, and glue, forming a sphere.
- Allow the glue to dry.
- Cut a hole through the center of the overlapped ends with the hole punch.
- Push about 2 in. (5 cm) of the pencil through the hole.
- Hold the pencil between your palms.
- Move your hands back and forth to make the paper sphere spin.

Results While the sphere is spinning, the top and bottom of the strips flatten slightly, and the center bulges.

Why? The spinning sphere has a force that tends to move the paper strips outward, causing the top and bottom to flatten. The earth, like all rotating spheres, bulges at the center and has some flattening at the poles. The difference between the distance around the earth at the equator and the distance around the earth at the poles is 42 miles (67.2 km).

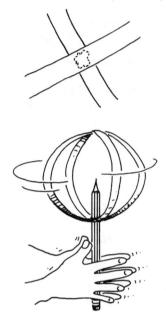

122. Precession

Purpose To demonstrate the movement of the earth's axis.

Materials modeling clay   round toothpick

Procedure
- Shape a piece of clay into a ball about the size of a marble.
- Push the toothpick through the center of the clay ball so that just the tip of the pick sticks out one side.
- Place the tip of the toothpick on a table.
- Twirl the long end of the pick with your fingers.
- Observe the movement of the top of the toothpick. *Note:* The ball spins poorly if the toothpick is not through the center or if the clay is not round.

Results As the clay ball spins, the top of the toothpick moves in a circular path.

Why? As the ball spins, there is a shifting of the weight because the ball is not perfectly round. The earth, like the clay ball, wobbles as it rotates because of the slight bulge at the equator. The earth's axis (the imaginary line through the poles of the earth) moves in a circular path as the earth wobbles. This movement is called *precession*. The top of the toothpick makes many revolutions as the clay ball spins, but it takes 26,000 years for the earth to wobble enough for its axis to make one complete turn.

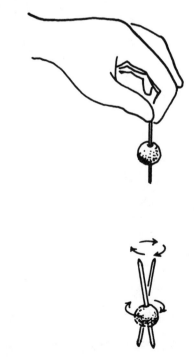

123. Wobbler

Purpose To demonstrate how the composition of the earth affects its motion.

Materials marking pen   1 hard-boiled egg
1 raw egg

Caution: Have an adult hard boil the egg.

Caution: Always wash your hands after touching an uncooked egg. It may contain harmful bacteria.

Procedure

■ Allow the boiled and raw eggs to stand at room temperature for about 20 minutes.

■ Mark numbers on each egg—boiled: 1; raw: 2.

■ Place both eggs on a table, and try to spin each egg on its side.

Results The hard-boiled egg spins easily and continues to spin for a few seconds. The raw egg wobbles and stops more quickly than the cooked egg.

Why? The material inside each shell affects the way it spins. The cooked egg has a solid content that spins with the shell. The liquid inside the raw egg does not start spinning with the movement of its shell. The outer shell motion does cause the liquid to move, but slowly. The sluggish movement of the liquid causes the egg to wobble and stop more quickly. Parts of the earth's mantle and outer core are liquid. The earth's interior is not solid, and like the egg, the earth wobbles during its rotations. Unlike the egg's wobbling, the earth's wobbling is very slight and takes many years for a noticeable change.

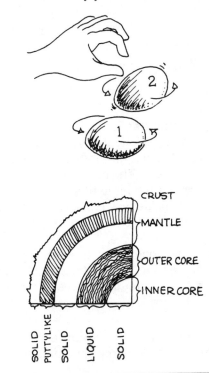

124. Day and Night

Purpose To determine the cause of the day and night cycle.

Materials table   dark shirt
flashlight   small hand mirror

Note: This experiment needs to be performed at night.

Procedure

■ Place the flashlight on a table and turn it on. The flashlight is to be the only light source in the room.

■ Stand about 12 in. (30 cm) from the flashlight wearing a dark shirt.

■ Slowly turn toward your left until you face away from the flashlight.

■ Hold the mirror at an angle to reflect light onto the back of your shirt.

■ Complete your turn and observe the front of your shirt as you turn.

Results A spot of light moves across your shirt toward your right side as you face the flashlight. Your shirt is dark when you turn away from the light until the reflected light from the mirror shines on the shirt. The reflected light is not as bright as the light directly from the flashlight.

Why? Your shirt represents the earth, the mirror the moon, and the flashlight the sun. Your turning imitates the rotation of the earth on its axis. As the earth turns toward the east, the light from the sun moves across the rotating earth. Daytime is experienced by the people on the side facing the sun, and reflected light from the moon brightens the side of the earth turned away from the sun. The nighttime is very dark when the moon is not in position to reflect the sun's light onto the earth.

125. Twilight

Purpose To determine why the sky is not dark as soon as the sun sinks below the horizon.

Materials quart (liter) jar   eyedropper
shoe box   spoon
milk   scissors
flashlight   adult helper

Procedure
- Fill the jar with water.
- Add one drop of milk to the water and stir.
- Ask an adult to cut a hole in the bottom of a shoe box next to the end. The hole should be round and large enough for the jar to fit in.
- Turn the box upside down and ask an adult to cut a hole in the box's side large enough to fit the flashlight.
- In a darkened room, turn the flashlight on and place it through the hole in the side of the box.
- Stand the jar of water in the hole in the upturned bottom of the box.

Results The water in the jar above the surface of the box has a pale blue-gray appearance.

Why? Light is composed of different waves of color. When blended together, they appear as white light. Each wave of colored light is a different size. The larger waves pass through the glass unaffected by the small particles of milk throughout the water. Blue light waves are small enough to be scattered by the milk particles. Some of the scattered light enters the water in the upper section of the glass, causing it to have a bluish-gray color. *Twilight* is the time just after the sun sinks below the horizon. The sky is not dark at twilight because the light from the sun, like the light from the flashlight, is scattered by dust particles and gas molecules in the earth's atmosphere.

126. Salty

Purpose To determine how salt beds are formed.

Materials glass bowl, 2 qt. (2 liter)
measuring cup, 1 cup (250 ml)
measuring spoon, tablespoon (15 ml)
table salt

Procedure
- Stir together in the bowl 1 cup (250 ml) of water and 4 tablespoons (60 ml) of salt.
- Allow the bowl to sit undisturbed until all the water evaporates. This may take 3 to 4 weeks.

Results Cubic crystals line the bottom of the bowl, with white frosty deposits on the inner sides of the bowl.

Why? Beds of salt are believed to have formed from shallow ponds that were close enough to the ocean to collect salt water and were then cut off from the sea. Slow evaporation of the water in the pond, as in the bowl, left behind clear cubic salt crystals called halite. Climbing clumps of frosty salt are formed where water rises up the sides of the pond or container, and salt in the solution crystallizes as the

water quickly evaporates. This fast drying does not allow the salt molecules to move into position to form cubic crystals. The random depositing of the salt molecules produces the frosty crystals.

127. Needles

Purpose To demonstrate how crystals form.

Materials   black construction paper
scissors
lid from a large jar
measuring cup, 1 cup (250 ml)
Epsom salts
measuring spoon, tablespoon (15 ml)

Procedure
- Cut a circle from the black paper that will fit inside the lid. Place the paper in the lid.
- Fill the measuring cup with water (250 ml).
- Add 4 tablespoons (60 ml) of Epsom salts to the water and stir.
- Pour a very thin layer of the mixture into the lid.
- Allow the lid to stand undisturbed for one day.

Results Long needle-shaped crystals form on the black paper.

Why? The Epsom salts molecules move closer together as the water slowly evaporates from the solution. The salt molecules begin to line up in an orderly pattern and form long needle-shaped crystals. The salt molecules stack together like building blocks, and the shape of the molecules determines the resulting shape of the crystal.

128. Bubbles

Purpose To demonstrate a positive test for limestone.

Materials   3 seashells   glass
vinegar

Procedure
- Fill a glass one-quarter full with vinegar.
- Add the seashells.

Results Bubbles start rising from the seashells.

Why? Vinegar is an acid and seashells are made of limestone, a mineral. Limestone chemically changes into new substances when in contact with an acid. One of the new substances formed is carbon dioxide gas, and it is the bubbles of this gas that are seen rising in the glass of vinegar. Acid can be used to test for the presence of limestone in rocks. If limestone is present in a rock, bubbles form when an acid touches the rock.

129. Crunch

Purpose To demonstrate the formation of metamorphic rocks.

Materials 20 flat toothpicks   book
          table

Procedure

- Snap the toothpicks in half, but leave them connected.
- Pile the toothpicks on a table.
- Place the book on top of the toothpick pile and press down.
- Remove the book.

Results The toothpicks are pressed into flat layers.

Why? The toothpicks flatten into layers under the pressure of the book. In nature, the weight of rocks at the surface pushes down on rock and dirt beneath, forcing them to flatten into layers. Rocks formed by great pressure are called *metamorphic rock.*

130. Sedimentary Sandwich

Purpose To demonstrate a sedimentary rock formation.

Materials 2 slices of bread
          crunchy peanut butter
          jelly
          knife, for spreading
          plate

Procedure

Note: Do this before lunch.

- Lay one slice of bread on a plate.
- Use the knife to spread a layer of peanut butter on the slice of bread.
- Add a layer of jelly on top of the peanut butter layer.
- Place the second slice of bread on top of the jelly layer.
- Eat the sandwich.

Caution: Never taste anything in a laboratory setting unless you are sure that there are no harmful chemicals or materials. This experiment is safe.

Results A sandwich with a series of layers has been constructed.

Why? Sedimentary rocks are formed from loose particles that have been carried from one place to another and redeposited. These rocks usually are deposited in a series of layers similar to the layers in the sandwich. Each layer can be distinguished by differences in color, texture, and composition. The oldest layer and lowest bed is deposited first and the youngest layer is at the top. The layers over a period of time become compacted and cemented together to form solid rock structures.

131. Line-Up

Purpose To demonstrate that some minerals have a definite cleavage line.

Materials paper towels

Procedure
- Try to rip a single sheet of a paper towel from top to bottom.
- Turn another sheet of paper towel and try to tear it from side to side.

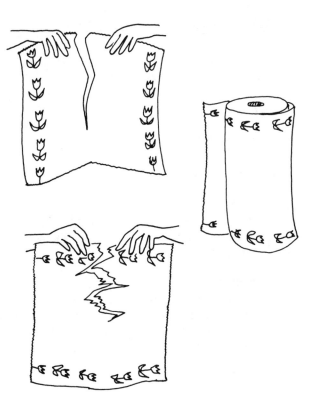

Results The paper will tear easily in one direction but not in the other.

Why? Paper towels are made on a wire screen, creating a straight line in one direction. Pulling on the paper attacks the weakest point. The parallel lines on the paper made by the wire screen are thinner than the rest of the paper, and thus the paper rips easily down one of these lines. Jagged and irregular tears result when the paper is pulled in the opposite direction. This is like cutting minerals, such a diamonds, along cleavage lines. The mineral splits smoothly and easily *along* the lines where the molecules line up, but it can smash into irregular pieces if hit *across* the cleavage line.

132. Folds

Purpose To demonstrate how compressional forces affect crustal movement.

Materials 4 paper towels   glass of water

Procedure
- Stack the paper towels on a table.
- Fold the stack of paper in half.
- Wet the paper with water.
- Place your hands on the edges of the wet paper.
- Slowly push the sides of the paper toward the center.

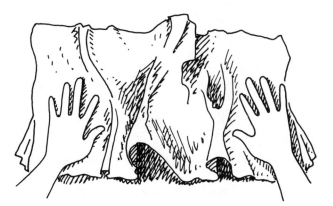

Results The paper has many folds.

Why? Your hands push the sides of the paper toward the center. Parts of the paper fold over so that it fits into the smaller space provided. When forces from opposite directions push against sections of the earth's crust, the compressed land is squeezed into new shapes called folds. The upper surface of this folded land has a wavelike appearance.

133. Easy Over?

Purpose To demonstrate the pressure required to fold the earth's crust.

Materials 1 sheet of newspaper

Procedure
- Fold the paper in half.
- Continue to fold the paper as many times as you can.

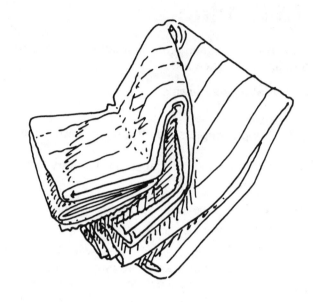

Results The paper becomes more difficult to fold. After the sixth or seventh folding, you will be unable to bend the paper.

Why? With each folding, the amount of paper doubles. After 7 foldings, there are 128 sheets. The earth's crust, like the paper, requires a small amount of pressure to fold thin, lighter layers on the surface. Tremendous amounts of pressure are required to fold over large, denser sections of land.

134. Slower

Purpose To determine why seismic waves move slowly through sand.

Materials paper towel
paper core from roll of paper towels
uncooked rice
rubber band

Procedure
- Cover the end of the paper core with one paper towel.
- Secure the paper towel to the tube with the rubber band.
- Fill the tube with rice.
- Use your fingers to push down on the rice. Try to push the rice down and out through the paper towel.

Results The rice is not pushed through the bottom of the tube. The rice moves very little.

Why? Sand particles, like the rice, move in all directions when pushed. Vibrations from seismic waves move more slowly through sand because the forward energy of the wave moves in different directions as the sand particles move outward in all directions.

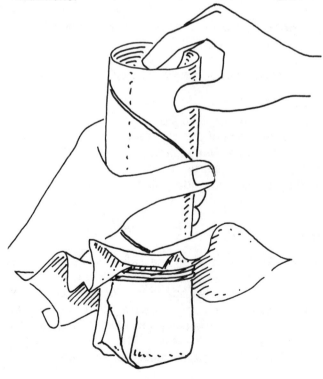

135. Quick

Purpose To determine the effect of different materials on the speed of p-waves (primary waves) produced by earthquakes.

Materials ruler   masking tape
              string   table
              scissors

Procedure
- Measure and cut a 30-in. (60-cm) length of string.
- Tape one end of the string to a table.
- Hold the free end of the string and stretch the string.
- Strum the stretched string with your finger. Listen.
- Wrap the end of the string around your index finger.
- Place the tip of your finger in your ear.
- Strum the stretched string with your fingers.

Results The sound is much louder when you put your finger in your ear.

Why? The vibrations from the string travel faster through the string attached to a solid than through the air. Primary waves, *p-waves,* are the first recorded vibrations from an earthquake. These waves travel as compression waves similar to sound waves. P-waves move faster when traveling through dense materials—materials that have their molecules close together. The speed of p-waves gives clues to the density of the materials through which they travel.

136. Ripples

Purpose To demonstrate how seismic waves give clues to the content of the earth's interior.

Materials bowl, 2 qt. (2 liter)   pencil
              glass soft-drink bottle

Procedure
- Fill the bowl about one-half full with water.
- Set the bottle in the center of the bowl of water.
- Tap the surface of the water several times near the side of the bowl with a pencil.

Results Waves ripple out from where the pencil touches the water. The waves hit the bottle and most are reflected back toward the pencil.

Why? The pencil vibrates the water, sending out waves of energy, but the waves are not able to move through the bottle. *S-waves* are secondary waves that arrive after the faster primary waves (p-waves). Both these waves are produced by earthquakes. S-waves are slower and have less energy than p-waves. These less energetic waves can move through solids but not through liquids. The s-waves move through the solid part of the earth but, like the water waves hitting the bottle, are reflected back by earth's liquid core. P-waves travel through the center of the earth, but s-waves are reflected back, which indicates that the inner part of the earth is in liquid form.

137. Covered

Purpose To demonstrate the effect of rain on hills with and without ground cover.

Materials 3 large shallow baking pans
table
modeling clay
ruler
2 cups of soil
quart (liter) bowl filled with a mixture of leaves, grass, and small twigs
1 drinking glass

Procedure
■ Place a shallow baking pan on a table.
■ Use clay to position two pans so that they are raised about 2 in. (5 cm) at one end, with their other ends resting inside the pan on the table as in the diagram.
■ Spread one cup of soil across the top section of the pans.
■ Cover the soil on one of the pans with the mixture of grass, leaves, and small twigs.
■ Hold a tilted glass full of water about 6 in. (15 cm) above the uncovered soil and allow the water to slowly pour onto the soil.

■ Repeat the procedure, on the covered soil.
■ Compare the amount of soil collected at the bottom of each elevated pan.

Results More soil washes away from the uncovered soil.

Why? Unprotected soil dissolves in the flowing water and moves down the pan. In nature, leaves, grass, and small twigs provide a protective covering. This covering holds the soil in place and soaks up water that might wash away the soil. Plants that grow in the soil provide even more protection because their roots help hold the soil in place. The washing away of soil is called *erosion.*

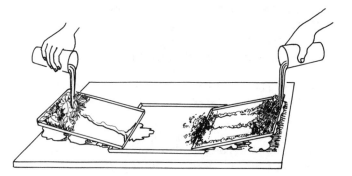

138. Rock Eater

Purpose To demonstrate the effect of acid on statues.

Materials chalk   glass
vinegar

Procedure
■ Fill a glass one-quarter full with vinegar.
■ Add a piece of chalk to the glass.

Results Bubbles start rising from the chalk. Small pieces start to break off, and finally the chalk totally breaks apart.

Why? Vinegar is an acid and acids slowly react chemically with the chalk. The piece of chalk is made of limestone, a mineral that quickly changes into new substances when touched by an acid. One of the new substances is the gas seen rising in the vinegar, which is carbon dioxide gas. Acids affect all minerals, but the change is usually slow. The slow deterioration of statues and building fronts is due to the weak acid rain that falls on the statue. If the stone is limestone or has limestone in it, the deterioration is more rapid. Some stones are more resistant to the attack acid.

139. Run Off

Purpose To demonstrate how rain affects topsoil.

Materials dirt
red powdered tempera paint
measuring spoon, teaspoon (5 ml)
stirring spoon
funnel
wide-mouthed jar, 1 qt. (1 liter)
coffee filter paper
measuring cup, 1 cup (250 ml)

Procedure

- Add ¼ teaspoon (1.25 ml) of red tempera paint to ¼ cup (75 ml) of dirt. Mix thoroughly.
- Set the funnel in the jar.
- Place the coffee filter inside the funnel.
- Pour the colored sand into the paper filter.
- Add ¼ cup (75 ml) of water to the funnel.
- Observe the water dripping into the jar.
- Pour this water out of the jar and add another ¼ cup (75 ml) of water to the funnel.

Results The liquid dripping out of the funnel is red.

Why? The red paint represents nutrients in topsoil that are soluble in water. Nutrients dissolve in rainwater and feed the plants growing in the soil. If the rain is too heavy, the water runs across the land, taking the dissolved nutrients with it. Excessive rains can leave the topsoil lacking in necessary nutrients.

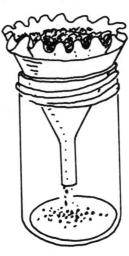

140. Fly Away

Purpose To determine how moisture affects land erosion.

Materials paper hole punch
baking pan
sheet of paper
water
shallow
bowl of

Procedure

- Cut about 50 paper circles from the paper with the paper hole punch.
- Place the paper circles in the pan at one end.
- Blow across the paper circles.
- Wet your fingers in the bowl of water and sprinkle the water over the paper circles. You want the paper to be damp.
- Blow across the paper circles again.

Results The dry paper particles easily move to the opposite end of the pan and some fly out of the pan. The wet paper does not move easily.

Why? Loose, lightweight particles can be picked up by the wind and carried for long distances. Flyaway surface particles that are easily supported by the wind are commonly found in deserts and along shorelines. The damp paper circles stick together and are too heavy for your breath to lift. Damp land areas and those covered by vegetation are not as easily eroded by the wind, because, like the damp paper, the materials are too heavy to be lifted by the wind.

141. Crack-Up

Purpose To determine if freezing water causes rock movement.

Materials drinking straw
modeling clay
glass of water
freezer

Procedure
- Place one end of the straw into the glass of water.
- Fill the straw by sucking the water into it.
- Hold your tongue over one end to prevent the water from escaping while you insert a clay plug into the open end of the straw.
- Remove your tongue and plug the end with clay.
- Lay the straw in the freezer for 3 hours.
- Remove the straw and observe the ends.

Results One of the clay plugs has been pushed out of the straw and a column of ice is extending past the end of the straw.

Why? Water, unlike most substances, expands when it freezes. When water gets into cracks in and around rocks, it can actually move or break the rock when it freezes. The expansion of the freezing water is enough to push apart weak points in the rocks. This is the main cause of potholes in the streets.

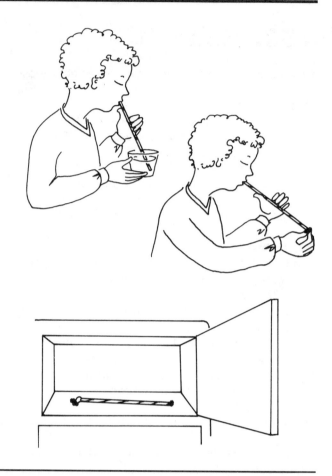

142. Holding

Purpose To determine how much pressure air has.

Materials 1 yardstick (meter stick)
table
1 sheet of newspaper

Procedure
- Place the measuring stick on a table so that half of the stick extends over the edge of the table.
- Fold a sheet of newspaper in half four times.
- Place the folded paper over the end of the measuring stick that is lying on the table.
- With your index finger, tap the end of the measuring stick.
- Observe the movement of the stick and folded paper.
- Unfold the sheet of newspaper and spread it over the measuring stick so that the paper lies flat along the table's edge.
- Tap the end of the measuring stick with the same force as before.
- Again observe the movement of the newspaper and measuring stick.

Results The newspaper is more difficult to lift when spread out than when folded.

Why? The weight of the folded and flat newspaper is the same. It is the pressure of the air on the paper that prevents it from rising. More than 250 miles (156 km) of air extending upward from the top of the paper presses the paper against the table. This column of air above the paper pushes down with a force of 15 lb. per square inch (1 kilogram per square centimeter). The average force on the surface of the folded paper is 578 lb. (263 kg). Laying the paper flat produces a surface about 16 times as large, and thus the pressure of the air is 16 times as great, or 9,248 lbs. (4,208 kg).

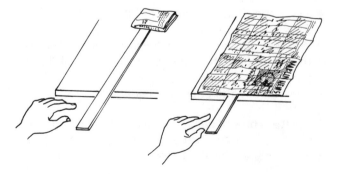

143. Rhythmic

Purpose To demonstrate how a gentle breeze can move heavy objects.

Materials string wide-tipped marking pen
scissors masking tape
ruler table

Procedure
- Cut a piece of string about 18 in. (45 cm) long.
- Tie one end of the string to the top of the marking pen.
- Tape the free end of the string to the top edge of a table with the pen hanging about 12 in. (30 cm) below the table's top.
- Kneel on the floor with the suspended pen about 12 in. (30 cm) in front of your face.
- Blow as hard as possible toward the pen.
- Observe the height the pen moves.
- Stop the pen from moving.
- Blow on the pen with a small puff of breath.
- Wait until the moving pen begins its swing away from your face and hit it with a small puff of breath. Do this 10 times.
- Again observe the height the pen moves.

Results The pen moves to a greater height when hit with small puffs of breath at the beginning of its swing than with one hard blast of breath.

Why? The *amplitude* (height) of any swinging object can be greatly increased by rhythmically applying a gentle push. Every object has a *natural vibration* (rate at which it can move back and forth). Applying a force at the same time an object starts its vibration is similar to "pumping" a swing at just the right time in each cycle; both increase the amplitude of motion.

144. Sprayer

Purpose To demonstrate how air pressure can be used to produce a spraying fountain.

Materials 1 nail, 16-penny size 2 straws
hammer modeling clay
adult helper green food
ruler   coloring
2 pint (500 ml) baking dish
  jars, one with a lid

Procedure
- Ask an adult to use the hammer and nail to make two holes in the lid.
- Push one straw through a hole so that 2 in. (5 cm) extends above the lid. (Straw A in the diagram.)
- Push the second straw through the other hole in the lid so that about 2 in. (5 cm) extends inside the lid. (Straw B in the diagram.)
- Use small pieces of modeling clay to seal the opening between the straw and the lid.
- Fill one jar half full with water and screw on the lid.
- Fill the second jar with water and add enough food coloring to turn it dark green.
- Set the jar of colored water in a baking dish.
- Turn the jar with the straws through the lid upside down with the shortest straw beneath the colored water in the jar.
- Observe the ends of the two straws.

Results Colored water rises and sprays out of straw A inside the closed jar. Water from the closed jar runs out of straw B and into the open baking dish.

Why? *Gravity* (the downward pull toward the center of the earth) pulls the water out of the closed jar and down through straw B. As the water leaves, the air in the jar spreads out, and the air pressure inside the closed jar is reduced. The air pressure outside the closed jar is now greater than the air pressure inside the jar. The air pushing down on the colored water forces the water up and out of straw A. The result is a spraying fountain inside the closed jar.

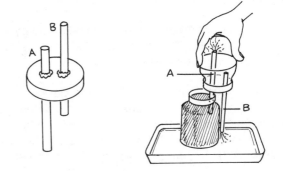

145. Spacey

Purpose To demonstrate that air takes up space.

Materials bowl, 2 qt. (2 liter)
small cork
clear drinking glass

Procedure
- Fill the bowl one-half full with water.
- Float the cork on the water's surface.
- Hold the glass above the floating cork.
- Press the open mouth of the glass down into the water.

Results The surface of the water with the floating cork is pushed down.

Why? The pocket of air inside the glass prevents the water from entering the glass, so the water with the floating cork is forced down below the level of the water outside the glass.

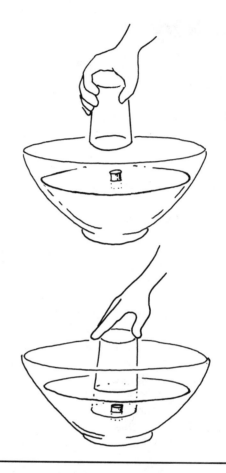

146. Straw Drill

Purpose To demonstrate the strength of air.

Materials 1 raw potato   2 plastic drinking straws

Procedure
- Place the potato on a table.
- Hold the straw at the top, leaving the top open.
- Raise the straw about 4 in. (10 cm) above the potato.
- Quickly and with force stick the end of the straw into the potato.
- Hold your thumb over the top of the second straw.
- Again raise the straw about 4 in. (10 cm) above the potato, and with force stick the straw into the potato.

Results The open-ended straw bends, and very little of the straw enters the potato. The closed straw cuts deeply into the potato.

Why? Air is composed mainly of the gases nitrogen, oxygen, and carbon dioxide. These gases are invisible, but the results of their pressure can be observed. Fast-moving air (wind) can apply enough pressure to destroy large buildings. The trapped air inside the straw makes the straw strong enough to break through the skin of the potato. The push of the air against the inside of the straw prevents it from bending. The pressure of the air increases as the plug of potato enters and compresses the air.

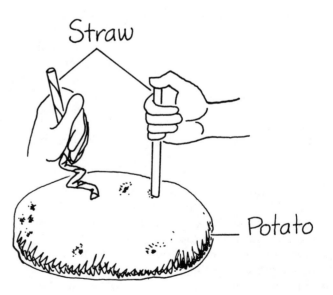

Straw

Potato

147. Drippy

Purpose To demonstrate 100% humidity.

Materials baking pan   sponge
             table   eyedropper

Procedure
- Fill the baking pan with water and set the pan on a table.
- Place the sponge on a table.
- Fill the eyedropper with water from the baking pan.
- Squeeze one drop of water from the eyedropper onto the sponge.
- Pick the sponge up with your hands and observe the bottom of the sponge.
- Place the sponge in the pan of water. Turn the sponge over in the water a couple of times.
- Again pick the sponge up with your hands, holding it above the pan of water.
- Observe the bottom of the sponge.

Results With one drop of water, the bottom of the sponge remains dry. Water drips out of the sponge after it is allowed to soak in the water.

Why? Air can be compared with the sponge in that they both can hold water. One drop of water in the sponge made very little difference, but soaking the sponge allowed it to become *saturated* (completely filled with water). Water dripped out of the sponge when it was unable to hold any more water. Air, like the sponge, can be saturated with water when it is filled to its capacity. *Relative humidity* is the amount of water in the air compared with its capacity. When the air is saturated, it is said to have a 100% humidity.

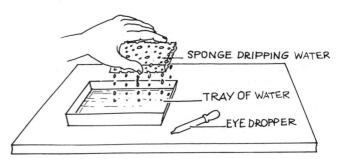

148. Up and Down

Purpose To demonstrate how a thermometer works.

Materials outdoor thermometer   ice cube
             cup

Procedure
- Hold the bulb of the thermometer between your fingers.
- Observe the level of the liquid in the thermometer.
- Fill the cup with water. Add an ice cube and stir.
- Place the bulb of the thermometer in the cold water.
- Observe the level of the liquid in the thermometer.

Results Holding the bulb between your fingers caused the liquid in the thermometer to rise. The liquid lowered in the thermometer column when the bulb was placed in cold water.

Why? Heat from your fingers increases the temperature of the liquid inside the thermometer. As the liquid is heated, it expands and rises in the thermometer tube. The cold water removes heat from the liquid in the thermometer. As the liquid cools, it contracts and moves down the tube. Outdoor thermometers are used to measure the temperature of air. Any increase or decrease in the heat content of air causes the liquid inside the thermometer to expand or contract, thus indicating the temperature of the surrounding air.

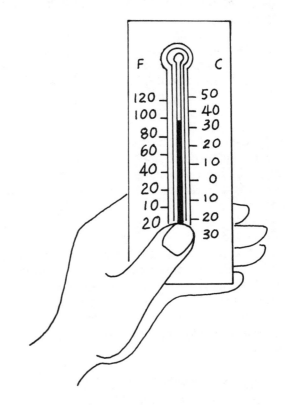

149. Cloud Watcher

Purpose To determine wind direction by use of a nephoscope.

Materials paper   compass
outside table   marking pen
mirror

Procedure

- Try this experiment on different days when the sky has separate clumps of moving clouds.
- Lay a sheet of paper on an outside table.
- Place a mirror in the center of the paper.
- Use a compass to determine the direction of north. Mark the direction on the paper with the marking pen.
- Look into the mirror and watch the image of the clouds as they move cross the mirror.
- Record the directions that the clouds are coming from.

Results The image of the clouds moves across the mirror.

Why? The direction and speed of surface winds are changed by obstructions such as trees and buildings.

This is why meteorologists and weather forecasters seek information about wind in the upper air. The instrument that you have made is called a *nephoscope*. It allows you to observe drifting clouds in order to determine the direction of wind in the upper air. Winds are named for the direction they come from. A north wind comes from the north and blows south.

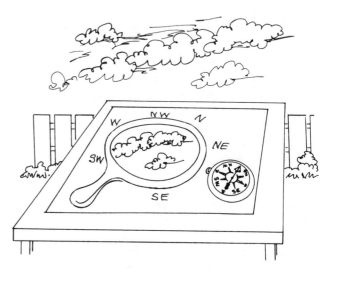

150. Wet Air

Purpose To demonstrate the use of hair in measuring humidity.

Materials cellophane tape   marker
straight strand of   pencil
hair about 5 in.   large glass jar
(12 cm) long   glue
flat toothpick

Procedure

- Use a small piece of tape to secure one end of the strand of hair to the center of the toothpick.
- Color the pointed end of the toothpick with the marker.
- Tape the free end of the hair strand to the center of the pencil.
- Place the pencil across the mouth of the jar with the toothpick hanging inside the jar. If the toothpick does not hang horizontally, add a drop of glue to the light end to balance the toothpick.
- Place the jar where it will be undisturbed.
- Observe the directions that the toothpick points for 1 week.

Results The toothpick changes direction.

Why? You have made a hair *hygrometer*. Hygrometers are instruments used to measure humidity, the amount of water in air. The hair stretches when the humidity increases; with a lower humidity, the hair shrinks. The stretching and shrinking of the hair pulls on the toothpick, causing it to move.

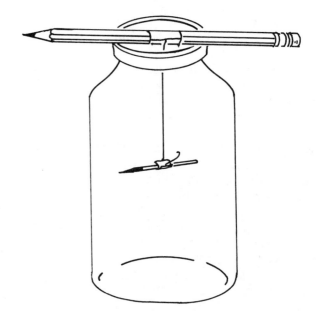

151. Crackle

Purpose To demonstrate how static electricity can be used to indicate humidity levels.

Materials clean, dry, oil-free hair   plastic comb

Procedure
- This experiment needs to be performed on several different days and the results noted.
- Be sure that your hair is clean, dry, and oil-free.
- Briskly comb your hair.

Results On some days, a crackling sound is heard as you comb your hair and on other days no sound is heard.

Why? Electrons are rubbed from the hair and onto the comb. Sound waves are produced when the electrons jump from the comb through the air and back to the hair. The crackling sound is heard best when the air is cool and dry and not heard at all when the air is warm and wet. Wet air contains many molecules of water that provide stepping-stones for the electrons to use when they move through the air. As the air becomes dryer, the number of water molecules decreases, so the electrons have a longer distance to jump when returning from the comb to the hair. The electrons clump together until the combined amount of their energy is great enough to move them across the span. The movement of these groups of electrons through the air produces the crackling sound.

152. How Big?

Purpose To collect and compare raindrop sizes.

Materials 1 sheet of black construction paper
umbrella

Procedure
- On a rainy day, stand under an umbrella while holding the sheet of black construction paper so the rain can hit it.

    Note: You can stand under any protective covering and hold the paper out into the rain.

    Caution: DO NOT do this experiment when there is lightning and thunder.
- Collect at least 20 drops of rain.
- In a dry area, observe the paper.

Results There will be different sizes of water spots on the paper.

Why? Raindrops are not all the same size. A drop of rain is made up of water molecules clinging together. Small raindrops have fewer molecules of water, and as more molecules of water stick together, the drop gets bigger.

153. Mover

Purpose To demonstrate how differences in *density* (a scientific way of comparing the "heaviness" of materials) cause water to move.

Materials   adult helper
                1 empty plastic cola
                  bottle, 1 liter size
                scissors
                4 ice cubes

                spoon
                blue food
                  coloring
                measuring cup
                  (250 ml)

Procedure
- Ask an adult to cut a plastic cola bottle in half.
- Fill the bottom of the cola bottle half full with cold water from a faucet and add 4 ice cubes. Stir the water with a spoon to cool it, then remove the ice.
- Fill the measuring cup with warm water from the faucet. Add enough blue food coloring to produce a dark blue liquid.
- Use the top section of the cola bottle as a funnel by turning it upside down and placing it inside the bottom section of the bottle.
- Tilt the cup so that half of the warm, blue water slowly runs into the cola bottle funnel.
- Observe the container for 2 minutes before pouring the remainder of the colored water into the funnel.

Results The blue water fills the funnel. Some of the colored water moves out of the neck of the funnel but quickly rises to the surface.

Why? Cold water is denser than warm water. This difference in density occurs because cold water *contracts* (gets closer together) and warm water *expands* (moves farther apart). This makes a drop of cold water heavier because there are more molecules of water in it than in a drop of warm water. Dense cold water settles in the bottom of the bottle as it does in the ocean, while the less dense warm water rises.

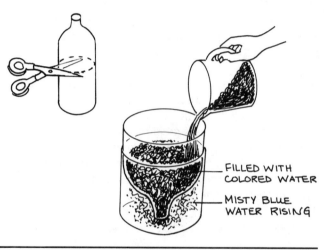

FILLED WITH COLORED WATER

MISTY BLUE WATER RISING

154. Subs

Purpose To demonstrate how air is used to lift submarines.

Materials   bowl, 2 quart (liter)
                clear plastic drinking glass, 7 oz. (210 ml)
                flexible drinking straw

Procedure
- Fill a bowl with water.
- Turn a glass on its side and push it beneath the surface of the water in the bowl. You want to fill the glass with as much water as possible.
- Keep the mouth of the glass beneath the water as you turn the glass so that it sits upside down on the bottom of the bowl.
- Raise the glass slightly with your hand and slip the end of a straw under the rim of the glass.
- Support the glass with your hand, but do not restrict its movement.
- Exhale through the straw.

Results As you exhale through the straw, water moves out of the glass and the glass rises to the surface of the water.

Why? Filling the glass with water makes it heavy enough to sink and rest on the bottom of the bowl. Your exhaled breath pushes water out of the glass. The weight of the gas in your breath is lighter than that of water. The glass is more *buoyant* (tending to float) when filled with gas than when filled with water. Submarines contain tanks that when filled with water cause the craft to sink. To surface, the water in the tanks is replaced with air, making the ship more buoyant.

155. Bobber

Purpose To demonstrate the movement of water molecules in waves.

Materials small balloon   bathtub
             rock   scissors
             string   ruler

Procedure
- Inflate the balloon to the size of a lemon.
- Attach the balloon to a rock with a 18-in. (45-cm) length of string.
- Fill the bathtub with about 6 in. (15 cm) of water.
- Set the rock in the center of the tub. The balloon should float on the surface with about 6 in. (15 cm) of extra string to allow it to move away from the rock.
- At the end of the tub, push your hand back and forth in the water for about 30 seconds to produce water waves.
- Observe the movement of the floating balloon.

Results The balloon moves in a circle around the sunken rock.

Why? It appears that water waves move forward,

but the actual water molecules are moving up and down in a circle. The movement of floating objects on a wave will be in a circle, with the diameter of the orbit equal to the height of the waves.

156. Bump!

Purpose To demonstrate the forward movement of wave energy.

Materials book   6 marbles

Procedure
- Lay the book on a flat surface such as a table or the floor.
- Open the book and place 5 of the marbles in the book's groove. Push the marbles tightly together and position the group in the center of the book.
- Place the free marble about 1 in. (3 cm) from the group of marbles, and thump it with your finger so that it moves forward and bumps into the end marble of the group.

Results The thumped marble stops when it strikes the end marble, and the marble on the opposite end of the group moves away from the group.

Why? The thumped marble has kinetic energy (energy of motion). Upon contact, this energy was transferred to the stationary marble, which transferred it to the marble next to it. Each marble transfers the energy to the next marble until the end

marble receives it and moves forward. Any one of the marbles would have moved forward had it not been blocked by another marble. Water waves appear to move forward, but actually only the energy is transferred from one water molecule to the next, and each water molecule remains in relatively the same place. Like the end marble, the water near the beach moves forward, since there is nothing holding it back.

157. Sinker

Purpose To determine how density affects water movement.

Materials   glass bowl, 2 qt. (2 liter)
                table salt
                measuring cup (250 ml)
                measuring spoon, tablespoon (15 ml)
                blue food coloring

Procedure
- Fill the cup about three-quarters full (200 ml) with water.
- Add 6 tablespoons (90 ml) of salt to the water and stir.
- Pour in drops of food coloring to make the water a very deep blue color.
- Fill the bowl one-half full with water.
- Observe the bowl from the side as you slowly pour the blue, salty water down the side of the bowl.

Results The colored water sinks to the bottom of the bowl, forming waves under the clear water above it.

Why? A density current is the movement of water due to the difference in the density of water. All sea water contains salt, but when two bodies of water mix, the water with the most salt will move under the lighter, less salty water.

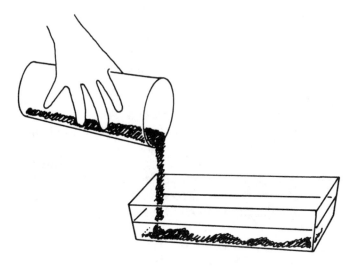

158. Twirler

Purpose To demonstrate the effect of the earth's rotation on wind and water currents.

Materials   construction paper   ruler
                scissors   eyedropper
                pencil

Procedure
- Cut an 8-in. (20-cm) diameter circle from the construction paper.
- Push the point of the pencil through the center of the circle.
- Place a drop of water on top of the paper near the pencil.
- Hold the pencil between the palms of your hands and twirl the pencil in a counterclockwise direction.

Results The water drop swirls around the paper in a clockwise direction.

Why? The free-moving water is thrown forward, and the spinning paper moves out from under the water. Wind and water currents in the Northern Hemisphere are turned toward the right because of the rotation of the earth. Like the spinning paper, the moving earth moves out from under the unattached air and water, causing them to change direction. The deflection in the motion of objects due to the earth's rotation is called the *coriolis effect*.

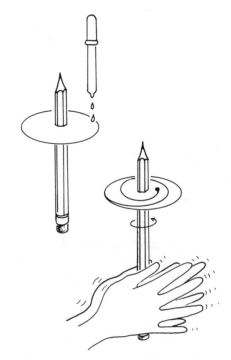

159. Hydrometer

Purpose To demonstrate how salt content is measured.

Materials jar, 1 qt. (1 liter)
modeling clay
table salt
measuring spoon, tablespoon (15 ml)
cap from a pen

Procedure

■ Fill the jar three-fourths full with water.
■ Put enough clay in the pen's cap so that it sinks when placed in the jar of water.
■ Add 1 tablespoon (15 ml) of salt to the water and stir.
■ Observe any change in the position of the cap.
■ Continue to add 1 tablespoon (15 ml) of salt at a time until 5 tablespoons (75 ml) have been added.
■ Observe the position of the cap in the water after each tablespoon of salt has been added.

Results The cap rises in the water as more salt is added.

Why? The upward push of the water on the cap is called the *buoyancy force.* This force increases with the weight of the water. Fresh water (water without salt) is less dense than salty water. As the salt content of the water increases, the water gets denser and has a greater buoyancy force, which lifts the cap higher in the water. The floating cap acts as a hydrometer, an instrument used to determine the salt content of water.

160. Slosh!

Purpose To determine how the shape of shorelines affects the height of tides.

Materials square baking pan   pie pan
round baking pan   outdoor water
source

Procedure

Note: This is an outdoor activity.
■ Fill each container to overflowing with water.
■ Pick up one pan at a time and walk forward with the container held in front of you.

Results The water spills more readily out of the square pan than out of the round baking pan or pie pan.

Why? Tides are the rise and fall of ocean waters and the entire ocean is affected from top to bottom. The difference in the rise and fall of the water is observed only along the shorelines. The pans represent shorelines of different shapes. The pie pan has a low, gently sloping side, and the square pan is more irregular than the round containers. Tides on low, gently sloping shores move in and out with little change.

Exceptionally high tides occur along irregularly shaped shorelines. The Bay of Fundy in Nova Scotia rises as much as 42 ft. (13 m) during its high tide.

V
Physics

161. Streamers

Purpose To charge an object with static electricity.

Materials scissors   ruler
              tissue paper   comb

Procedure
- Measure and cut a strip of tissue paper about 3 in. × 10 in. (7.5 cm × 25 cm).
- Cut long, thin strips in the paper, leaving one end uncut (see diagram).
- Quickly move the comb through your hair several times. Your hair must be clean, dry, and oil-free.
- Hold the teeth of the comb near, but not touching, the cut end of the paper strips.

Results The thin paper strips move toward the comb.

Why? Static means stationary. *Static electricity* is the buildup of negative charges, which are called *electrons.* Matter is made up of atoms, which have electrons spinning around a positive center called the *nucleus.* Moving the comb through your hair actually rubs electrons off the hair and onto the comb. The side of the comb that touched your hair has a build-up of electrons, making that side negatively charged.

The paper strip is made of atoms. Holding the negatively charged comb close to the paper causes the positive part of the atoms in the paper to be attracted to the comb. This attraction between negative and positive charges is strong enough to lift individual strands of paper.

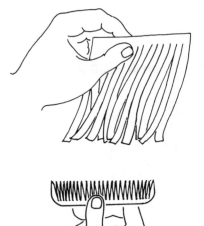

162. Snap

Purpose To demonstrate how *static* charges produce sound.

Materials clear plastic sheet
              scissors
              ruler
              modeling clay
              large paper clip
              piece of wool: a scarf, coat, or sweater made of 100% wool will work

Procedure
- Measure and cut a plastic strip about 1 in. × 8 in. (2.5 cm × 20 cm).
- Use the clay to stand the paper clip upright on a table.
- Wrap the wool around the plastic strip and quickly pull the plastic through the cloth. Do this quickly at least three times.
- Immediately hold the plastic near the top of the paper clip.

Results A snapping sound can be heard.

Why? Electrons are rubbed off the wool and onto the plastic. The electrons clump together until the addition of their energy is great enough to move them across the span of air between the plastic and the metal clip. The movement of the electrons through the air produces sound waves, resulting in the snapping sound heard.

163. Suspended Airplane

Purpose To use magnetic force to suspend a paper airplane.

Materials tissue paper   steel straight pin
scissors   bar magnet
ruler
sewing thread, 12 in. (30 cm)

Procedure

■ Measure and cut a small wing about 1 in. (2.5 cm) long from the paper.
■ Insert the pin through the center of the paper wing to make an "airplane."
■ Tie the thread to the head of the pin.
■ Place the magnet on the edge of a table with the end of the magnet extending over the edge of the table.
■ Place the airplane on the end of the magnet.
■ Slowly pull on the string until the airplane is suspended in the air.

Results The airplane remains airborne as long as it stays close to the magnet.

Why? The strength of attraction between two magnets depends on how orderly the *magnetic domains* (clusters of atoms that behave like tiny atoms) are in the magnets. The atoms in the pin are randomly arranged before the pin touches the magnet. The number of atoms that arrange themselves into clusters (domains) and line up in the pin when it is placed on the magnet depends on the strength of the magnet. The pin and magnet both have magnetic properties. They pull on each other with enough force to overcome the downward pull of gravity, which allows the airplane to remain suspended.

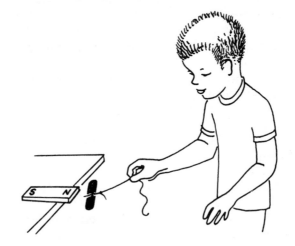

164. Force Field

Purpose To demonstrate the pattern of magnetic force fields around magnets of different shapes.

Materials magnets, a variety—round, bar, U-shaped
iron filings: Remove the iron filings from a magnetic disguise set found at a toy store.
paper cup
notebook paper

Procedure

■ Pour the iron filings into the paper cup.
■ Place the magnets on a table.
■ Cover the magnets with a sheet of paper.
■ Sprinkle a thin layer of iron filings on the paper over the magnets.
■ Observe the iron filing patterns.

Results The iron filings form a pattern of lines around the magnets. The long magnet has a buildup of filings around both ends.

Why? A *magnetic field* is the area around a magnet in which the force of the magnet affects the movement of metal objects. The iron filings are pulled toward the magnets when they enter the magnetic field. The magnetic force increases as the filings near the magnet. The force field has equal strength around the round magnet, but the force fields at the ends of rectangular magnets are always stronger than the force fields in the middle of the magnets.

165. Electromagnet

Purpose To demonstrate that an electric current produces a magnetic field.

Materials wire, 18-gauge, insulated, 1 yd. (1 m)
long iron nail   paper clips
6-volt battery   adult helper

Procedure
- Wrap the wire tightly around the nail, leaving about 6 in. (15 cm) of free wire on each end.
- Have an adult strip the insulation off both ends of the wire.
- Secure one end of the wire to one pole of the battery.
- Touch the free end of the wire to the other battery pole while touching the nail to a pile of paper clips.
- Lift the nail while keeping the ends of the wire on the battery pole.
- When the nail starts to feel warm, disconnect the wire end you are holding against the battery pole.

Results The paper clips stick to the iron nail.

Why? There is a magnetic field around all wires carrying an electric current. Straight wires have a weak magnetic field around them. The strength of the magnetic field around the wire was increased by coiling the wire into a smaller space, placing a magnetic material—the nail—inside the coil of wire, and increasing the electrical flow through the wire—attaching a battery. The iron nail became magnetized and attracted the paper clips.

166. Keeper

Purpose To determine how metals affect a magnetic field.

Materials 4 small paper clips   bar magnet
aluminum foil   steel spatula

Procedure
- Lay the paper clips on a table and cover them with a sheet of aluminum foil.
- Set the magnet on the foil over the clips.
- Raise the magnet and observe any movement of the clips.
- Position the clips so that they lay under the spatula.
- Set the magnet on top of the spatula.
- Lift the spatula with the magnet and observe any movement of the clips.

Results The magnet attracts the paper clips through the aluminum foil. The magnet does not attract the paper clips through the steel spatula.

Why? The magnetic force field passes through the aluminum, but the steel blade restricts the movement of the force field. The steel blade is attracted to the magnet, but the metal provides another path for the magnetic field. This new path is through and around the steel blade. The steel keeps the lines of force closer to the magnetic field, acting as a barrier to other magnetic materials.

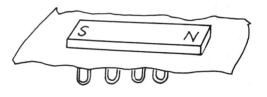

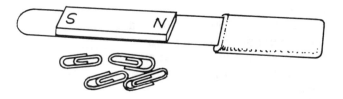

167. Tilt

Purpose To demonstrate that objects in water have a different weight than they do in air.

Materials heavy string table
scissors masking tape
ruler marking pen
2 washers 3 drinking glasses,
pencil 8 oz. (250 ml)

Procedure
- Measure and cut two strings 12 in. (30 cm) long.
- Tie one string around each end of the pencil.
- Tie one washer to the end of each string.
- Cut a string about 24 in. (60 cm) long.
- Tie one end of the string around the center of the pencil and tape the free end to the edge of a table.
- Move the position of the supporting string on the pencil until the pencil hangs parallel with the edge of the table. The washers should be about 4 in. (10 cm) above the floor.
- Use tape and a marking pen to label two glasses as A and B.
- Set the empty glasses on the floor so that one washer hangs inside each glass.

- Fill a third glass with water from the faucet and slowly pour the water into glass A.

Results When the water level touches the washer, the washer rises, the pencil tilts, and the washer in the empty glass is lowered.

Why? *Gravity* pulls everything toward the center of the earth. This downward pull on the washers is referred to as their *weight*. The glasses appear to be empty but are actually filled with air. In air, the weight of the two washers is the same. Placing one of the balanced washers in water decreases its downward pull (weight) and causes the pencil to tilt toward the heavier side. The upward force exerted by water is called *buoyancy*.

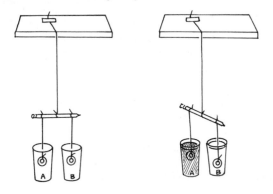

168. Risers

Purpose To determine how the buoyancy of a substance can be changed.

Materials drinking glass modeling clay
club soda

Procedure
- Fill the drinking glass three-quarters full with soda.
- Immediately add 5 tiny balls of clay one at a time. The clay pieces must be about the size of a rice grain.
- Wait and watch.

Results Bubbles collect on the clay. The clay pieces rise to the surface, spin over, and fall to the bottom of the glass, where more bubbles start to stick to them again.

Why? The soda contains carbon dioxide, which forms bubbles that stick to the clay. The clay balls initially sink because their weight is greater than the upward buoyant force. The gas bubbles act like tiny balloons that make the balls light enough to float to the surface. The carbon dioxide bubbles are knocked off at the surface, and the balls again sink to the bottom until more bubbles stick to them.

169. Shapely

Purpose To determine if shape affects the strength of an object.

Materials 3 sheets of typing paper
          cellophane tape
          light books, about 1 lb. (454 g)

Procedure
- Fold the paper sheets into three shapes by following these steps:
  - Shape A—fold one sheet in thirds and tape the edges together.
  - Shape B—fold one sheet into fourths and tape the edges together.
  - Shape C—roll one sheet into a cylinder and tape the edges together.
- Stand each paper shape on a flat table.
- Place one book at a time on top of each shape until it collapses.
- Record the number of books that each paper shape can support.

Results The rolled paper holds more books.

Why? *Gravity* (a pull toward the center of the earth)

pulls each book downward, and the paper structures push upward. If the upward push is less than the downward pull of gravity, the book crushes the paper structure. The open paper cylinder is the strongest of the shapes tested because the *weight* (force of gravity) of the supported book(s) is evenly distributed through the paper pillar.

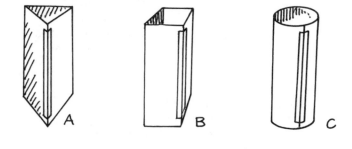

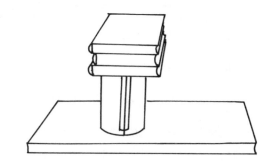

170. Up Hill

Purpose To determine the effect that an object's center of gravity has on motion.

Materials 2 yardsticks (meter sticks)
          3 books, each at least 1 in. (2.5 cm) thick
          masking tape
          2 funnels of equal size

Procedure
- Put two books 30 in. (90 cm) apart on the floor.
- Place the remaining book on top of one of the other books.
- Position the yardsticks on top of the books to form a V shape with the open part of the letter on the double book stack.
- Tape the bowls of the funnels together.
- Place the joined funnels at the bottom of the track formed by the yardsticks.

Results The funnels roll up the hill.

Why? The funnels are not defying the laws of gravity. Actually, as the joined funnels move, their *center of gravity* (the point where the weight is equally

distributed) moves downward. Notice that the center of the joined funnels gets closer to the floor as it moves along the raised yardsticks.

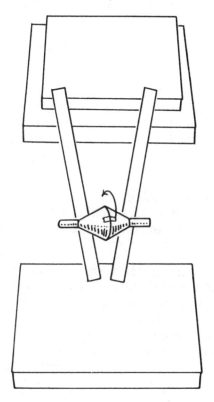

171. Timer

Purpose To determine how the length of a pendulum affects the time of each swing.

Materials string
washer
scissors
ruler
table

heavy book
stopwatch or watch with
  a second hand
helper

Procedure

- Measure and cut a string the height of the table.
- Tie one end of the string to the washer, and use tape to attach the other end of the string to the end of the ruler.
- Lay the ruler on the table with about 4 in. (10 cm) of the ruler extending over the edge, and the string hanging freely.
- Lay the book on top of the ruler to hold it in place.
- Pull the washer to one side and release it.
- Ask your helper to start the timer as you count the number of swings in 10 seconds.
- Shorten the string by one-fourth its length.
- Pull the washer to one side, release it, and count the number of swings in 10 seconds as your helper records the time.

Results The number of swings doubles with the shorter string.

Why? Galileo has been credited for discovering the relationship between the length of a pendulum and the time of its swing. The story told is that he observed the swinging of a great lamp while in church and timed the swings by comparing it with his pulse beat. He later discovered that the time of a swing depends on the length of the pendulum and that the time decreases by one-half if the string is one-fourth the original length.

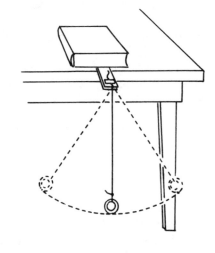

172. Over the Edge

Purpose To demonstrate that the center of gravity is the balancing point of an object.

Materials string, 12 in. (30 cm)
yardstick (meter stick)
hammer (wooden-handled hammer
  works best)

Procedure

- Hold the ends of the sting together and tie a knot about 2 in. (5 cm) from the ends.
- Insert the hammer and yardstick through the loop.
- Position the end of the yardstick on a table's edge.
- The handle of the hammer must touch the yardstick and the head of the hammer will extend under the table.
- Change the position of the hammer until the whole unit—yardstick, string, and hammer—balances.

Results The unit balances with only a small amount of the yardstick touching the table.

Why? The hammer, string, and yardstick all act as a single unit with a *center of gravity.* The center of gravity is the point where any object balances. The dashed line in the diagram allows you to visualize the center of gravity. The heavy hammer head counterbalances the weight on the left side of the balancing point.

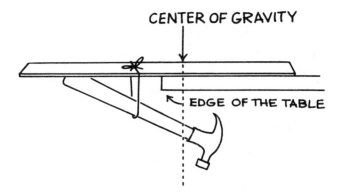

CENTER OF GRAVITY

EDGE OF THE TABLE

173. Balancing Act

Purpose To determine the center of gravity point.

Materials modeling clay   1 flat toothpick
2 metal forks   drinking glass or
wide-mouthed jar

Procedure
- Make a ball of clay about the size of a large marble.
- Insert the tip of one of the forks into the clay ball.
- Insert the second fork at about a 45-degree angle from the first fork.
- Insert the pointed end of the toothpick in the clay between the forks.
- Place the end of the toothpick on the edge of the glass. Move it further over the glass until the forks balance.

    Note: Decrease the angle between the forks if they will not balance.

Results There is one point at which the toothpick supports the weight of both forks and the clay.

Why? The angle of the forks spreads their weight so that there is one place on the toothpick where all

of the weight seems to be located. This spot is called the *center of gravity.*

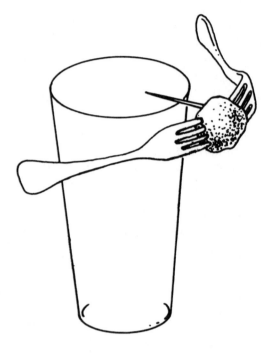

174. Lift Off

Purpose To demonstrate the effect of a kite's tail.

Materials 1 sheet of notebook paper   string
scissors   ruler
cellophane tape

Procedure
- Measure and cut a 2-in. × 12-in. (5-cm × 30-cm) strip from the sheet of paper.
- Use tape to attach an 18-in. (45-cm) length of string to one end of the strip.
- Hold the free end of the string and whip the paper back and forth in front of you.
- Cut a ¼-in. × 12-in. (0.5-cm × 30-cm) strip from the paper and attach it with tape to the free end of the wider strip.
- Again move the strip back and forth in front of you.

Results The paper twirls around, but when the small strip is attached, the movement is smoother.

Why? The paper moves forward at an angle, causing the air to flow faster over the top side. Fast-moving air has a lower pressure around the moving stream. Thus, more uplift is exerted on the bottom of the

strip. The angle of the paper is not constant, causing changes in the pressure along with a turbulent air flow across the strip. These changes make the strip twist and rotate. The paper tail makes the angle more constant. Therefore, there is a smoother flow of air across the paper and less twisting.

175. Paper Flop

Purpose To demonstrate the effect of speed on air pressure.

Materials 2 books of equal size
ruler
1 sheet of notebook paper
1 drinking straw

Procedure
■ Position the books 4 in. (10 cm) apart on a table.
■ Lay the sheet of paper across the space between the books.
■ Place the end of the straw just under the edge of the paper.
■ Blow as hard as you can through the straw.

Results The paper flops down toward the table when air is blown under it.

Why? Air was pushing equally on all sides of the paper before you blew through the straw. As the speed of a flow of air increases, the sideways pressure of the air decreases. Forcing a stream of fast-moving air under the paper reduces the upward pressure on the paper. The air pushing down on the paper is greater than the air pushing up, thus the paper flops down.

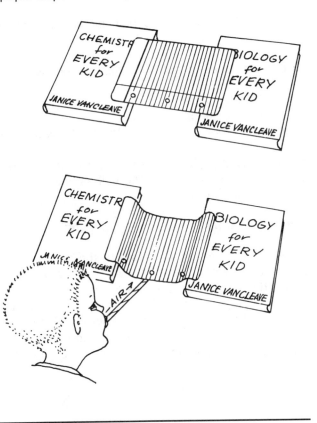

176. Swish

Purpose To demonstrate how a perfume sprayer works.

Materials drinking glass
scissors
two flexible drinking straws

Procedure
■ Fill the glass with water.
■ Cut one straw so that the top of the flexible section stands ½ in. (1 cm) above the water's surface. Stand this straw in the water.
■ Hold the second straw horizontally so that its end is pointed across the top of the other straw. Use the ridges on the straw standing in the water as a support.
■ Blow hard through the horizontal straw.

Results Water rises in the standing straw and is blown out in a mist.

Why? The faster air moves, the lower the pressure around the flow of air. As the air from the straw moves across the top of the standing straw, the pressure inside the standing tube is lowered. Atmospheric pressure in the room pushes down on the surface of the water in the glass, forcing the water to the top of the straw, where it is blown out in a mist. Squeezing on a perfume sprayer produces the same situation. Air is forced across a tube and the perfume rises due to the reduced pressure inside and is thus sprayed outward by the moving air.

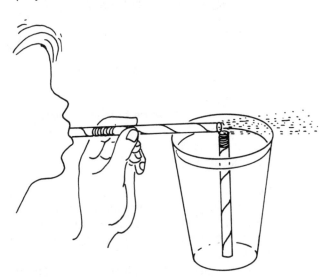

177. Floating Ball

Purpose To demonstrate how air speed affects flight.

Materials small funnel   table tennis ball

Procedure
- Turn the funnel upside down.
- Hold the table tennis ball in the funnel with your finger.
- Start blowing into the narrow end of the funnel.
- Remove your finger from the ball as you continue to blow into the funnel.

Results The ball floats inside the funnel.

Why? The faster the air passes by the ball, the less pressure it exerts upon the ball. The air pressure above the ball is less than the pressure under it, so the ball is held up by air. The pressure of moving air explains the upward lift on the wings of aircraft. When the air flows faster over the top of the wing than below, there is an upward push called *lift*.

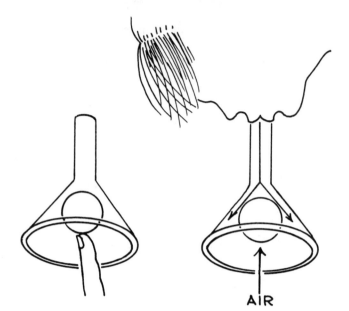

178. One Sided

Purpose To demonstrate the advantage of using a Moebius strip as a connecting belt for wheels.

Materials adult helper
2 large empty thread spools
ruler
board, 2 in. × 4 in. × 16 in. (5 cm × 10 cm × 40 cm)
2 large nails, 10-penny size
hammer
scissors
3 ft. (1 m) of white butcher or wrapping paper
green marking pen
masking tape

Procedure
- Ask an adult to position the empty spools 12 in. (30 cm) apart on the board, securing them with nails as shown in the diagram. The spools should turn easily around the nails.
- Cut a strip of paper 1 in. × 36 in. (2.5 cm × 100 cm) and use a marking pen to color one side of the strip.
- Wrap the paper strip around the spool, give one end of the strip a half turn, cut off excess paper,

and tape the ends to make the loop fit snugly around the thread spools.
- Use your hand to turn one of the thread spools in a clockwise direction.
- Observe the direction of motion of both spools, and the color of the paper passing over the spools.

Results Both thread spools turn in a clockwise direction. Each time the taped ends appear, the color of the paper changes.

Why? The spools and paper strip act as belted wheels. Wheels (spools) connected by a belt rotate in the same direction. Each time the taped ends appear, the twist in the strip causes the paper to flip over, exposing the opposite side. Untwisted belts wear out faster on the inside than the outside. Using a Moebius strip (a loop with a twist) allows the belt to wear evenly on both sides, and thus it wears more slowly.

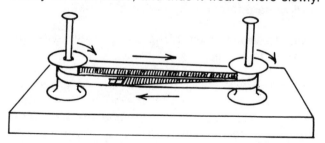

179. Turn Around

Purpose To determine how a seesaw can be balanced with one person much heavier than the other.

Materials
yardstick (meter stick)
table
string
scissors
masking tape
15 coins
(pennies)
2 paper cups

Procedure
- Hang a yardstick (meter stick) from the edge of a table by a 36 in. (1 m) string tied around its middle. Use tape to secure the string to the table.
- Use string to hang a cup with 5 coins on one end of the measuring stick and a cup with 10 coins on the opposite end of the stick.
- Move the cup with 10 coins toward the center of the stick until the stick balances.

Results The cup with 5 coins is twice as far from the center supporting string as the cup with 10 coins.

Why? The place where the stick is held up is its *fulcrum*. The weight of an object turns the stick around its fulcrum. A seesaw, like the stick, balances when the turning effect on one side equals the turning effect on the other side. This can be achieved with objects of different weights by placing the lighter object farther from the fulcrum and the heavier object closer to the fulcrum.

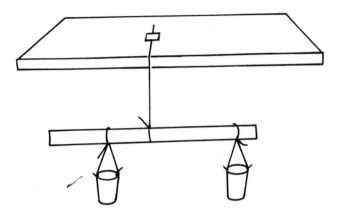

180. Weakling

Purpose To demonstrate a second-class lever.

Materials 2 round toothpicks

Procedure
- Place a toothpick across the back of your middle finger at the first knuckle and under the first and third finger.
- Try to break the toothpick by pressing down with your first and third fingers.
- Move the toothpick closer to the tips of your fingers.
- Again push down with your fingers to try to break the toothpick.

Results It is very difficult or impossible to break the toothpick when it is at the ends of your fingers.

Why? Your fingers act as a second-class lever similar to a nutcracker. The point of rotation or *fulcrum* is where the fingers join the hand. When the toothpick is placed furthest from the fulcrum, the force needed to break the toothpick is greatest. Placing the toothpick close to the fulcrum requires less effort—force—to break the wood.

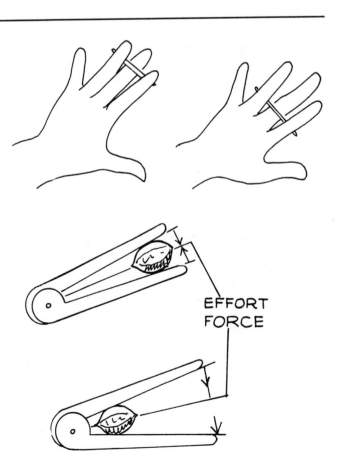

EFFORT FORCE

181. Tug of War

Purpose To demonstrate how easily things are moved with a machine.

Materials two brooms
rope or strong cord, 9 ft. (3 m)
2 helpers

Procedure
- Tie the rope to one broom handle.
- Wrap the rope around the broom handles three times while they are being held about 20 in. (50 cm) apart.
- Have your helpers try to keep the broom handles apart while you pull on the loose end of the rope.

Results You can move the broom handles together even though your helpers are trying to keep them apart.

Why? The brooms and rope act as a pulley system. Your force is multiplied by the number of ropes attached to the brooms; therefore, you have about five times the effort or force that is being exerted by each of your helpers.

182. Oops!

Purpose To demonstrate that due to inertia an object remains stationary.

Materials wagon   tennis ball

Procedure
- Place the tennis ball in the center of the wagon's bed.
- Quickly move the wagon forward.

Results When the wagon moves forward, the ball hits the back of the wagon.

Why? *Inertia* is a resistance to any change in motion. An object that is stationary remains that way until some force causes it to move.

The tennis ball is not attached to the wagon. Because of the ball's inertia, it remains stationary even though the wagon moves forward. The wagon actually moves out from under the stationary tennis ball.

183. Thump!

Purpose To demonstrate how forces affect inertia.

Materials drinking glass   clothespin
                  index card

Procedure
- Place the index card over the mouth of the glass.
- Place the clothespin on top of the card so that it is centered over the glass.
- Quickly and forcefully thump the card straight forward with your finger.
- Repeat the experiment several times.

Results The clothespin falls straight into the glass about half of the time; the other half of the time it flips over, landing upside down in the glass.

Why? Your finger applies force to the card, moving it forward. The card moves so quickly that it translates very little force to the clothespin. The pin falls straight down due to the pull of gravity when the card no longer supports it. If you do not hit the card straight forward with enough force, it pulls the bottom of the pin forward and gravity pulls the top of the pin down, causing the pin to flip before it lands.

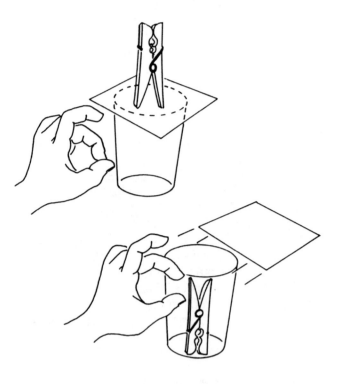

184. Moving On

Purpose To demonstrate how friction affects inertia.

Materials shoe box   10 round marking pens
                  scissors   balloon, 9 in. (20 cm)
                  adult helper   table
                  ruler

Procedure
- Ask an adult to cut a hole about ½ inch (1 cm) square in the center of the end of a shoe box.
- Lay the balloon inside the box with its mouth sticking out through the square hole in the end of the box.
- Inflate the balloon and hold the mouth of the balloon shut between your fingers.
- Place 10 round marking pens under the bottom of the shoe box on a table.
- Release the balloon.

Results As the balloon deflates, the box moves forward. It continues to move for a short distance after the balloon deflates.

Why? *Newton's First Law of Motion* states that an object will not change its motion unless an unbalanced force acts on it. This resistance that an object has to having its motion changed is called *inertia*. The box stays where you put it unless it is pushed. The deflating balloon gives the box a forward push. This unbalanced force starts the box moving, and it continues to move until a second force, *friction,* makes the box slow down and then stop. *Friction* is a force that pushes against a moving object, causing it to stop moving.

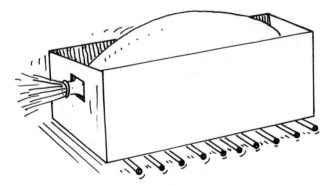

185. Spacer

Purpose To determine the size of a single hole needed to pour liquid out of a can.

Materials 3 empty soda cans   scissors
         paper towels   duct tape

Procedure

- Remove the opening tab from the tops of three soda cans.
- Fill the three cans with water from a faucet.
- Use paper towels to dry the tops of each can.
- Use the scissors to cut two strips of tape 1 in. (2.5 cm) square.
- Leave the opening in one of the cans uncovered (A).
- Cover three-fourths of the opening in one of the cans with one strip of tape (B).
- Use the second piece of tape to cover one-half of the opening in another can (C).
- Hold one can at a time over a sink. Tilt each can at the same angle.
- Observe any flow of liquid out of the cans.

Results The liquid quickly pours out of can A, no liquid pours out of can B, and the liquid dribbles out of can C.

Why? Water, like all liquids, takes up space, as does air. In order for the water to leave the cans, air must enter and take its place. The shape of the hole in an open soda can is long enough to allow the liquid to pour out the bottom part of the hole and air to enter at the top. Covering three-fourths of the hole prevents air from entering, and the liquid inside seals the hole. Covering only half the hole allows air to enter, but not continuously; some water has to pour out before the air can enter. This causes the water not to flow in a steady stream, but to dribble.

186. Shifter

Purpose To demonstrate transfer of energy between connecting pendulums.

Materials 2 chairs   scissors
         yardstick (meter stick)   2 washers
         string

Procedure

- Stand two chairs about 1 yard (1 m) apart.
- Attach a string to the tops of the chair backs to form a taut line between the chairs.
- Measure and cut two pieces of string 24 in. (60 cm) long and attach a washer to the ends of each string.
- Tie the free ends of the strings about 24 in. (30 cm) apart to the string between the chairs.
- As indicated in the diagram, use your hand to pull string A to the side so that it is straight and level with the top of the chairs.
- Release the string and allow it to fall.

Results String A swings back and forth, and as it swings, string B starts to move. As one string slows, the other increases in speed. This cycle continues to reverse itself until both strings are stationary.

Why? The hanging strings are *pendulums* (a rod or string with a weight attached to the end). The pendulums are attached to a central line; thus when one pendulum moves, the line moves and pulls on the second hanging pendulum. The amount of energy needed to move the strings is transferred back and forth through the connecting line. During the transfer of energy, one pendulum slows while the other increases in motion; at times, one pendulum has all the energy while the other pendulum remains stationary; with equal amounts of energy, their swings are the same height. Because of friction (resistance to motion), both pendulums finally stop swinging.

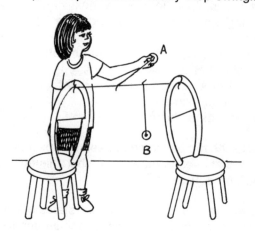

187. Balloon Rocket

Purpose To demonstrate how unbalanced forces produce motion.

Materials yardstick (meter stick)   2 chairs
drinking straw   balloon, 9 in.
scissors   (23 cm)
string   masking tape

Procedure

- Measure and cut a 4-in. (10-cm) piece from the drinking straw.
- Cut about 3½ ft. (4.5 m) of string.
- Thread the end of the string through the straw piece.
- Position the chairs about 4 ft. (4 m) apart.
- Tie the string to the backs of the chairs. Make the string as tight as possible.
- Inflate the balloon and twist the open end.
- Move the straw to one end of the string.
- Tape the inflated balloon to the straw.
- Release the balloon.

Results The straw with the attached balloon jets across the string. The movement stops at the end of the string or when the balloon totally deflates.

Why? *Newton's Law of Action and Reaction* states that when an object is pushed, it pushes back. When the balloon was opened, the walls of the balloon pushed the air out. When the balloon pushed against the air, the air pushed back and the balloon moved forward, dragging the straw with it. The string and straw keep the balloon rocket on a straight course.

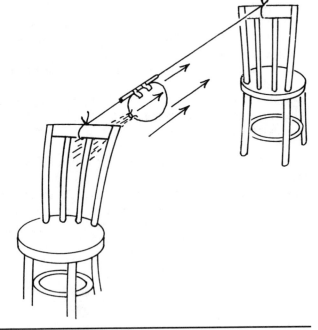

188. Helicopter

Purpose To determine how weight affects the rotation speed of a paper helicopter.

Materials notebook paper   pencil
scissors   3 paper clips
ruler

Procedure

- Fold and cut one sheet of paper in half lengthwise.
- Fold one of the halves in half lengthwise.
- Use a ruler to draw a triangle on one edge of the paper. The base will be 1 in. (3 cm) long and one side will be between the 4-in. and 6-in. (9 cm and 14 cm) marks on the ruler. See the diagram.
- Cut out the triangle. Cut through both layers of the paper.
- Open the paper and cut up the center fold to the point indicated on the diagram. This forms the two wings.
- Fold the tabs toward the center and attach a paper clip to the bottom.
- Fold the wings in opposite directions.
- Hold the helicopter above your head and drop it.
- Add different numbers of paper clips one at a time and drop the plane after each addition.

Results The rotation speed increases as the weight increases, but a point is reached where additional weight pulls down with such force that the wings move upward and the plane falls like any falling object.

Why? As the paper falls, air rushes out from under the wings in all directions. The air hits against the body of the craft, causing it to rotate. Increasing the weight by adding paper clips causes the helicopter to fall faster, and the amount of air hitting the craft's body increases. This increase in air movement under the wings increases the rotation speed.

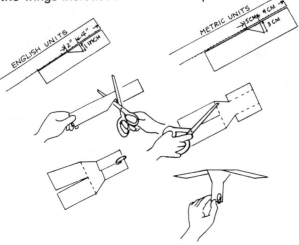

189. Right or Left?

Purpose To determine how wing position affects the direction of a paper helicopter's rotation.

Materials paper helicopter from Experiment 188

Procedure
■ Hold the helicopter above your head and drop it.
■ Observe the direction that the helicopter spins.
■ Bend the wings in the opposite direction and again drop the helicopter from above your head.

Results The helicopter spins counterclockwise when the right wing is bent toward you and turns clockwise when the wings are reversed.

Why? Air rushes out from under each wing in all directions as the helicopter falls. The air hits against the body of the craft, pushing it forward. Both halves of the body are being pushed in a forward direction, resulting in a rotation about a central point. The diagrams indicate direction of movement.

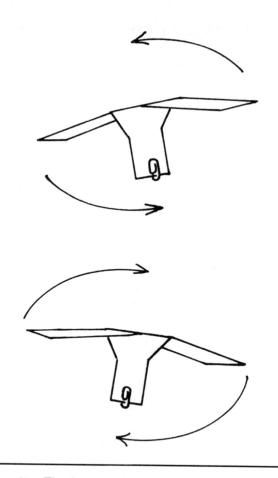

190. Paddle Boat

Purpose To demonstrate Newton's Law of Action and Reaction.

Materials
cardboard   rubber band
scissors   container of water at
ruler   least 4 in. (10 cm) deep

Procedure
■ Measure and cut a 4-in. (10-cm) square from the cardboard.
■ Shape the boat by cutting one side into a point and cutting out a 2-in. (5-cm) square from the opposite end.
■ Cut a paddle from the cardboard. Make it 1 in. × 2 in. (2.5 cm × 5 cm).
■ Loop the rubber band over the ends of the boat.
■ Insert the paddle between the sides of the rubber band.
■ Turn the cardboard paddle toward you to wind the rubber band.
■ Place the boat in the container of water and release the paddle.
■ Wind the rubber band in the opposite direction by turning the paddle away from you.
■ Place the boat in the water and release the paddle.

Results The boat moves forward with the first trial and backward when the paddle is turned in the opposite direction.

Why? *Newton's Law of Action and Reaction* states that when an object is pushed, it pushes back with an equal and opposite force. Winding the paddle caused it to turn and hit against the water. When the paddle pushed against the water, the water pushed back and the boat moved. The boat moved in the opposite direction to the paddle, changing direction when the paddle direction changed.

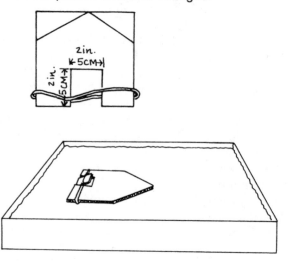

191. It's Alive

Purpose To demonstrate how an opaque projector works.

Materials shoe box
magnifying lens
scissors
adult helper
table
masking tape
modeling clay
index card
flashlight

Procedure

- Ask an adult to cut a hole large enough to hold the magnifying lens in the side of one end of a shoe box.
- Insert the magnifying lens in the hole, and use tape to secure it.
- Place the box on a table.
- Make a screen by using a piece of modeling clay to stand an index card on a table in front of the magnifying lens.
- Place the end of a flashlight in the corner of the box opposite the magnifying lens. Point the flashlight toward the opposite corner as in the diagram.
- In a darkened room, hold your left hand, fingers down, inside the box at the end opposite the magnifying lens.

- Move the box back and forth from the index card screen until a distance is found that produces the clearest image of your hand on the screen.
- Wiggle your fingers.

Results You can see an upside down, moving, color image of your left hand on the paper screen.

Why? Light from the flashlight reflects from your hand through the magnifying lens. The lens gathers the light and brings it into focus. At the *focal point,* an image, or picture, of the object exists and can be projected onto a screen. Light travels in a straight line, but when it hits the lens, it changes direction, causing the image to be upside down.

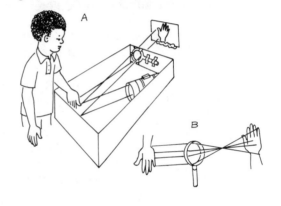

192. Polarized Light

Purpose To determine how polarized light moves.

Materials two pairs of polarized sunglasses

> *Note:* Be sure you are using polarized glasses.

Procedure

- Put one pair of glasses on.
- Observe how objects around you appear.
- Hold the second pair of glasses in front of your eyes.
- Slowly rotate the pair of glasses you are holding so that one lens turns in front of your right eye.
- Observe the quality of vision as you turn the glasses.

Results One pair of sunglasses seems to cut down glare and change the shade of objects. During the rotation of the second pair of glasses, the objects seen through the right eye got darker until finally nothing could be seen through the two lenses.

Why? A polarized lens has an endless number of parallel slits. Light waves moving in the same direction as the slits are allowed to pass through. Light

not moving in the same direction as the slits in the lens is blocked and cannot pass through.

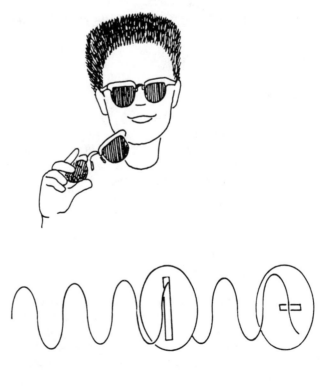

193. Swirls of Color

Purpose To separate light into colors.

Materials bowl of water, 1 qt. (1 liter)
bottle of clear fingernail polish

Procedure
- Place the bowl of water on a table away from direct lighting.
- Hold the brush from the polish bottle over the bowl of water and allow one drop of liquid polish to fall into the bowl.
- Watch the surface of the water. Move your head so that you see the surface from different angles.

Results A rainbow of colors is seen in the thin layer of fingernail polish on the surface of the water.

Why? The nail polish forms a thin film across the water. When light rays strike the film, part of each ray is reflected from the surface. Part of the ray goes through and is reflected off the bottom of the film. If the reflected rays overlap as they leave the film, colors are seen. The timing has to be just right for the reflected rays from the surface and bottom of the film to meet as they leave the film; if this does not happen, areas without colors are seen. This rainbow of colors is called a *spectrum*.

194. Backwards

Purpose To determine how a mirror affects the reflected image.

Materials hand mirror   pencil
4 books   paper

Procedure
- Support the mirror with the books.
- Place the paper under the edge of the mirror.
- Rest your chin on your hand so that you can see into the mirror, but so that your view of the paper where you will be writing is blocked.
- Look only into the mirror as you write your name so that it appears correctly in the mirror.
- Examine your writing.

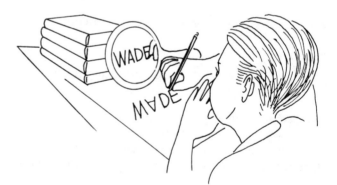

Results Most of and maybe all the letters are upside down.

Why? Because you are writing so that the letters are correct in the mirror, they are reversed on the paper. Most letters would be written upside down for this experiment except those that are symmetrical (the same on both sides) such as O, E, H, I, and B. These letters look the same with or without the mirror. The mirror gives you a reversed image.

195. Hot Band

Purpose To demonstrate energy changes.

Materials rubber band

Procedure
- Place the rubber band on your forehead and note the rubber band's temperature.
  Note: Your forehead is sensitive to heat and can therefore be your sensing device.
- Hold the rubber band between your thumbs and index fingers with your thumbs touching.
- Stretch the rubber band.
- Quickly touch the stretched band to your forehead.

Results The stretched rubber band feels warm.

Why? The rubber band is made of molecules coiled like a spring. Stretching the rubber band straightens the coils; they recoil when the band is released. You used *mechanical energy*—energy of moving things—to pull the coils of molecules apart, and the rubber band used energy to pull the coils back together. Some of the mechanical energy was changed into *heat energy.* Energy was needed to stretch the rubber band, and energy was needed to restore it to its original shape. If there were no changes in the molecular structure of the rubber band, the amounts of energy used to stretch and to recoil the rubber band would be the same. The energy changed from one form to another, but it was not lost. This is called *conservation of energy.*

196. Explosive

Purpose To determine why popcorn pops.

Materials unpopped popcorn
hot-air popcorn popper

Procedure
- Observe the shape and size of a few unpopped corn kernels.
- Ask an adult helper to assist you in setting up the popcorn popper.
- Observe the shape and size of the corn kernels as they are being heated.

Results The corn kernels change from small, hard, orange, kernels to large, soft, white, ball-shaped structures.

Why? The tough outside of the unpopped kernel is called the *pericarp.* This is the part that often gets stuck in your teeth when you eat popcorn. The inside is filled with starch that expands into the white, fluffy popcorn. The small amount of water inside the kernel makes the explosion possible. As the kernel is heated, the liquid water *evaporates*—changes to a gas. The gas expands and pushes so hard on the pericarp that it breaks and the starch tissue inside is blown outward. The pop noise is the sound of steam escaping and the pericarp breaking.

197. Bouncer

Purpose To determine if temperature affects the bounce of a rubber ball.

Materials tennis ball
yardstick (meter stick)
refrigerator with freezer

Procedure
- Hold the yardstick with one hand and place the ball at the top edge of the yardstick.
- Release the ball, and observe the height of the first bounce. Repeat three times to get an average of the bouncing height.
- Place the ball in a freezer for 30 minutes.
- Again measure the height that the ball bounces when released from the top of the yardstick.

Results The ball does not bounce as high when it is cold.

Why? Rubber is made of thousands of small molecules joined to form long chains. At room temperature, the chains easily push together and pull apart to make the ball bounce. The chains of molecules become rigid when the ball is chilled. The

flexibility of the chains of molecules allows the tennis ball to bounce. Playing tennis in cold weather would affect your game.

198. Boom!

Purpose To demonstrate the effect of solids on the speed of sound.

Materials clear plastic drinking glass
rubber band

Procedure
- Stretch the rubber band around the glass as shown in the diagram.
- Hold the bottom of the glass against your ear.
- Gently strum the stretched rubber band.

Results The sound heard is very loud.

Why? Sound is produced when objects vibrate. As the object moves back and forth, it hits against air and any other object near enough to be touched. When vibrations start air moving, the continuous ocean of air around you transfers the energy to your ears, and you register that sound has been produced. Vibrations move much more slowly through the air—a gas—than they do through liquids or solids. The vibrating rubber band causes the air around it to move, but the booming sound that you hear is because the solid plastic transmits the vibrations to your ear.

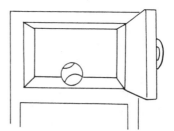

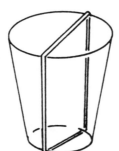

199. Straw Flute

Purpose To determine if the length of a flute affects the pitch of the sound it produces.

Materials drinking straw   ruler
scissors

Procedure
- Make a ½-in. (1.3-cm) cut on each side of the straw's end. This forms the reed part of the flute.
- Place the reed in your mouth.
- Push on the reed with your lips and blow. You may have to try several times and change the pressure of your lips in order to produce a sound.
- As you play the straw flute, cut the end of the straw off with the scissors and observe any change in pitch.

Results The *pitch* of the sound gets higher as the length of the straw decreases.

Why? The sound produced is due to the vibration of the straw and the air inside it. The longer the column of vibrating air inside the tube, the lower is the pitch of the sound.

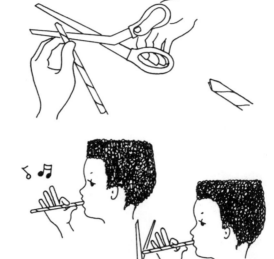

200. Clucking Chicken

Purpose To use a vibrating string to produce a sound.

Materials pencil
paper cup, 6.4 oz. (192 ml)
kite string, 24 in. (60 cm)
toothpick
sponge, rectangular kitchen sponge
water

Procedure
- Use the pencil to punch two holes about ½ in. (1.5 cm) apart in the bottom of the cup.
- Push the string through the holes and tie it on the outside of the cup.
- Insert the end of the string in one of the holes and pull it through so that the string hangs out of the cup.
- Place a toothpick under the loop of string on the outside of the cup with the ends of the toothpick extending over the edges of the cup.
- Cut a 1-in. × ½-in. (2.5-cm × 1.3-cm) section from the sponge.
- Tie the end of the string around the center of the piece of sponge.

- Wet the sponge with water.
- Wrap the wet sponge around the top of the string.
- Squeeze the sponge against the string as you move the sponge down the string using jerky movements.

Results A sound is produced like that of a clucking chicken.

Why? The water allows the sponge to move down the string, but there is enough friction to cause the string to vibrate, because the sponge skips and pulls at the string. This irregular touching on the string produces tiny taps that force the string's molecules to move back and forth. The vibrating string strikes the molecules in the cup, and the cup's molecules strike the air molecules, causing them to move back and forth in rhythm with the cup and string. The sound is made louder because the inside of the cup acts like a megaphone that concentrates the sound waves and sends them out in one direction.

Glossary

Acid: A material that tastes sour, neutralizes bases, and turns purple cabbage juice red.

Adsorbent: A solid to whose surface liquid and/or gas molecules adhere (stick).

Amplitude: Height of any swinging object.

Astrolabe: Instrument used to measure distances.

Atmosphere: Layer of air surrounding the earth.

Atom: The smallest part of an element. It contains a positive center with negative charges spinning around the outside.

Aurora Australis: Light display in the Southern Hemisphere. Gases in the earth's upper atmosphere glow when hit by charged particles in solar winds.

Aurora Borealis: Light display in the Northern Hemisphere. Gases in the earth's upper atmosphere glow when hit by charged particles in solar winds.

Auxin: A chemical that changes the speed of plant growth.

Base: A material that tastes bitter, neutralizes acids, and turns purple cabbage juice green and turmeric paper red.

Bioluminescence: Light produced by living organisms.

Buoyant force: The upward force that a liquid exerts on an object. The force is equal to the weight of the liquid that is pushed aside when the object enters the liquid.

Capillary action: The movement of a liquid in a thin tube due to the differences in pressure inside and outside the tube.

Catalase: An enzyme found in living cells.

Celestial: Relating to things in the heavens.

Centripetal force: The force pulling toward the center that keeps an object moving in a curved path.

Chemical reaction: The changing to new substances.

Colloid: A solution containing tiny undissolved particles that permanently remain suspended in the liquid.

Condensation: The change from a gas to a liquid by decreasing the heat content of the gas.

Constellation: A group of stars that, viewed from the earth, form the outline of an object or figure.

Core: The center part of an object.

Corona: Glowing gas layer around the outside of the sun.

Density: The measurement of the mass (weight) of a specific volume; the scientific way of comparing the "heaviness" of a material.

Diffusion: Spontaneous movement of molecules from one place to another resulting in a uniform mixture.

Eclipse: The blocking of light from a celestial body when another body comes between it and the observer.

Electrons: Negatively charged particles spinning around the atom's nucleus (the center part of every atom).

Emulsion: A combination of immiscible liquids.

Enzyme: A chemical found in living cells that changes the speed of the chemical reaction in the cells.

Erosion: Wearing away.

Evaporate: The change from a liquid to a gas by increasing the heat content of the liquid.

Fluid: Any substance that can flow.

Focal point: Place where an image of an object exists and can be projected onto a screen.

Friction: A force that pushes against a moving object causing it to stop moving.

Fulcrum: The point of rotation on a lever.

Galaxy: A large system of stars and other celestial bodies.

Gravity: The attraction between two objects because of their mass. The earth pulls everything toward its center.

Highlands: The mountainous regions on the moon.

Hygrometer: Instrument used to measure humidity.

Immiscible: The inability of two liquids to mix.

Inertia: Resistance to any sudden change in state, motion, or rest.

Inertia balance: Instrument used to measure the mass of an object. Because the balance works with or without gravity, it is used to measure mass in space.

Kinetic energy: Energy of motion having magnitude as well as direction.

Magnetic domain: Clusters of atoms that behave like tiny magnets.

Magnetic field: The area around a magnet in which the force of the magnet affects the movement of other magnetic objects.

Magnetic force field: Area around a magnet that attracts magnetic materials.

Magnetosphere: The area around the earth that is affected by the earth's magnetic field.

Maria: Flat plains on the moon.

Melanin: Special cells containing dark grains that produce skin color.

Metamorphic rock: Rocks that have been changed by heat, pressure, chemical actions, or a combination of these.

Molecule: The tiny particle produced by the linking of two or more atoms.

Molt: To shed the outer layer of feathers, fur, or skin.

Nephoscope: Instrument used to determine the direction of wind in the upper air.

Nucleus: The center of the atom, containing positively charged protons and neutral neutrons, which gives it an overall positive charge.

Orbit: The path of an object around another body; planets moving around the sun.

Osmosis: The movement of water from an area of great amounts of water to an area of lesser amounts of water.

Pendulum: A rod or string fixed at one end allowing it to swing freely to and fro.

Pericarp: The tough outer portion of a kernel of corn.

Photometer: An instrument used to measure the brightness of a light.

Photosynthesis: Food-making reaction in plants. It uses carbon dioxide, water, and sunlight to produce oxygen and sugar.

Phototropism: Plant growth in response to light.

Polarized lens: Allows light rays moving in one direction to pass through.

Precession: A slow change or wobble in the direction of the earth's axis.

Prism: Triangle-shaped piece of glass that bends the rays of light passing through it so that the light breaks into its separate colors, which is called a spectrum.

Proton: Positive particles in the nucleus of all atoms.

P-waves: Fast seismic waves that move, like sound waves, as compression waves. These waves can travel through liquids and solids.

Refracted: The change of speed of light as it moves out of one material and into another.

Relative humidity: The amount of water in the air compared with its capacity.

Respiration: A reaction in plants and animals that uses oxygen and sugar to produce carbon dioxide, water, and energy.

Retina: Back layer of the eyeball where images are focused by the lens.

Retrograde: The backward movement of an object such as the apparent backward motion of Mars.

Retroreflector: Instrument used by NASA to measure the distance from the earth to its moon.

Revolution: The time it takes for one celestial body to move around another one.

Rotation: Spinning around an axis; the earth's movement around its imaginary axis.

Rust: Combination of iron and oxygen called iron oxide; a reddish powder.

Satellite: A small object that circles a larger body.

Sedimentary rock: Rock made of layers of sediments that have been cemented together.

Semipermeable membrane: A material that allows different-sized materials to pass through it.

Solute: The material that breaks into smaller parts and moves throughout a solvent.

Solvent: The material that a solute dissolves in.

Solution: The combination of a solute and a solvent.

Spectrum: The colors found in white light—red, orange, yellow, green, blue, indigo, and violet.

Spore: A reproductive cell in some organisms such as mold.

Static electricity: A buildup of negative charges called electrons. Static means stationary.

Stomata: Pores in plant leaves.

S-waves: Seismic waves that move earth particles up and down as the wave energy moves forward. The wave can move only through solids.

Transpiration: Loss of water through plant pores, the stomata.

Triboluminescence: Light given off from crystals due to pressure.

Turgor pressure: Pressure of water inside plant cells.

Twilight: The time just after the sun sinks below the earth's horizon.

Uvula: Hanging piece of skin at the top of your throat.

Viscosity: The measurement of the thickness of a fluid or its resistance to flowing.

Volume: Space occupied by matter.

Vortex: Whirling liquid or gas with a cavity in the center toward which things are pulled. Examples are whirlpools, tornadoes, and waterspouts.

Weight: The amount of pull that gravity has on an object.

Wind: Movement of air.

Xylem: Tiny tubes in the stalk of a plant stem; transports water and food to the plant cells.

Index

**Get these fun and exciting books by Janice VanCleave
at your local bookstore, call toll-free 1-800-956-7739
or visit our Web site at: www.wiley.com/children/**

Janice VanCleave's Science for Every Kid Series

____Astronomy	53573-7	$11.95 US / 15.95 CAN
____Biology	50381-9	$11.95 US / 15.95 CAN
____Chemistry	62085-8	$11.95 US / 15.95 CAN
____Constellations	15979-4	$12.95 US / 15.95 CAN
____Dinosaurs	30812-9	$10.95 US / 15.95 CAN
____Earth Science	53010-7	$11.95 US / 15.95 CAN
____Ecology	10086-2	$10.95 US / 15.95 CAN
____Geography	59842-9	$11.95 US / 15.95 CAN
____Geometry	31141-3	$11.95 US / 15.95 CAN
____Human Body	02408-2	$11.95 US / 15.95 CAN
____Math	54265-2	$12.95 US / 15.95 CAN
____Oceans	12453-2	$12.95 US / 15.95 CAN
____Physics	52505-7	$12.95 US / 15.95 CAN

Janice VanCleave's Spectacular Science Projects Series

____Animals	55052-3	$10.95 US / 12.95 CAN
____Earthquakes	57107-5	$10.95 US / 12.95 CAN
____Electricity	31010-7	$10.95 US / 12.95 CAN
____Gravity	55050-7	$10.95 US / 12.95 CAN
____Insects & Spiders	16396-1	$10.95 US / 15.50 CAN
____Machines	57108-3	$10.95 US / 12.95 CAN
____Magnets	57106-7	$10.95 US / 12.95 CAN
____Microscopes & Magnifying Lenses	58956-X	$10.95 US / 12.95 CAN
____Molecules	55054-X	$10.95 US / 12.95 CAN
____Plants	14687-0	$10.95 US / 12.95 CAN
____Rocks & Minerals	10269-5	$10.95 US / 12.95 CAN
____Volcanoes	30811-0	$10.95 US / 12.95 CAN
____Weather	03231-X	$10.95 US / 12.95 CAN

Janice VanCleave's Science Bonanzas Series

____200 Gooey, Slippery, Slimy, Weird & Fun Experiments

	57921-1	$12.95 US / 16.95 CAN

____201 Awesome, Magical, Bizarre & Incredible Experiments

	31011-5	$12.95 US / 16.95 CAN

____202 Oozing, Bubbling, Dripping & Bouncing Experiments

	14025-2	$12.95 US / 16.95 CAN

Janice VanCleave's Play and Find Out About Science Series

____Play and Find Out About the Human Body

	12935-6	$12.95 US / 18.50 CAN

____Play and Find Out About Nature

	12940-2	$12.95 US / 16.95 CAN

____Play and Find Out About Math

	12938-0	$12.95 US / 18.50 CAN

____Play and Find Out About Science

	12941-0	$12.95 US / 16.95 CAN

Janice VanCleave's Guide to the Best Science Fair Projects

____Guide to the Best Science Fair Projects

	14802-4	$14.95 US / 19.95 CAN

Janice VanCleave's A+ Projects for Young Adults Series

____Biology	58628-5	$12.95 US / 17.95 CAN
____Chemistry	58630-7	$12.95 US / 17.95 CAN

Prices subject to change without notice.